OBSTACLE ILLUSIONS

Discovering How To Conquer Your Obstacles To
Create The Future You Have Always Dreamed Of

DAN SINGLETARY

OBSTACLE ILLUSIONS
Discovering How To Conquer Your Obstacles To Create The
Future You Have Always Dreamed Of

Copyright © 2023, Destiny Rising
ISBN-13: 979-8-9881861-0-6
Destiny Rising
www.DestinyRising.net

Dedication

I am humbled to dedicate this book to the one who has always been my guiding light and unwavering support. My wife and business partner, Theresa, embodies steadfastness and inspiration.

Theresa has been my anchor and a driving force behind our achievements. Her calm demeanor and structured approach have perfectly complemented my creative chaos, resulting in successful collaborations and exciting experiences we share together.

Without her support, this book would have remained a collection of ideas and notes. Her unwavering faith in me and countless cups of coffee together give me added strength on my journey.

Our partnership has been a testament to the power of support, creativity, and hard work. Perhaps this book will inspire and empower others to find their own Theresa and embark on countless adventures that will lead them to greatness together.

Table of Contents

Introduction.. 6

    B.B.A.A.L.L. and Intention 15

    Problem, Not Problem 23

Lies And Obstacle Illusions 26

Creation And Reality 26

    Creation 26

    Reality.. 27

    Filters 30

    Deletion 30

    Distortion... 31

    Generalization 32

    Not Your Map 34

    Stay On Your Mat.. 35

Living At Cause... 38

Attention And Energy 46

Layers Of the Mind 57

    The Conscious and Subconscious Mind........................ 57

    Environment... 60

    Behavior 62

    Potential 62

    Beliefs 64

    Values 66

Identity 67

Purpose 71

The Illusion of Labels 73

Internal Conflicts... 76

Unresolved Unresourceful Emotions 81

Acceptance And Creating Space............................. 86

Creating Space for Your Emotions........................... 90

T.I.M.E. Techniques... 93

The Impact of T.I.M.E Techniques........................... 94

Limiting Beliefs 97

Attachments 103

Attachment To Emotions 106

Attachment To the Past 108

Attachment To Outcomes.................................... 110

Fear.. 113

Calm... 122

Love 126

Next steps... 128

INTRODUCTION

Who is this book for?

This book is for people who are determined to overcome obstacles and strive to be better today than they were yesterday. It is written for those with an open mind and desire for personal growth.

We all encounter challenges in life that we need to conquer. Whether fear, lack of confidence, or unfavorable circumstances, our minds can deceive us into clinging to the past, fixating on the future, and neglecting the present. Often, we find ourselves living with regret or discontentment.

Do you aspire to overcome any obstacle that holds you back? Do you long for the power to change your life?

Successful people perceive their lives as stories because that's what they are! You are the main character and can reshape the narrative anytime you want. This book presents practical ways to transform your thoughts, reframe past experiences, and approach life with renewed perspective. This book is for you if you yearn to achieve something significant beyond mediocrity and seek true freedom. It is for those who want to live with passion, those tired of feeling stuck, and those ready to embrace life to its fullest and surpass its limitations. It is for those prepared to move past disempowerment. This book is for you.

Neuro-linguistic programming (NLP) is the field of study concerned with modeling the success of others and incorporating it into oneself or others. As Jim Rohn said, "Success leaves clues." much of what you will read in this book adopts an NLP perspective. I intend to provide you with new insights and information and offer familiar knowledge from fresh perspectives, enabling you to create your own future and live the life of your dreams. I firmly believe that you can hear something a million times, but it may not resonate until you encounter it in the right way, at the right time, from the right person. I hope to be that person for you.

It is no coincidence that you are reading this book. There is a reason behind it. Take a moment to contemplate these questions:

1.   What is truly important to me in overcoming obstacles and shaping my future?

2.   If I possessed the knowledge to create my future, how would I utilize it to positively change my life?

One of my mentors has a mission to impact as many people as possible and empower them to lead extraordinary lives. He achieves this through a ripple effect, where one person influences ten, ten influence a hundred, a hundred influence a thousand, and so on. You and I are two ripples in a much larger pond. Many NLP enthusiasts undergo NLP training because they discover the ability to help others in ways they never thought possible. After finishing this book, I encourage you to share it with others who you believe it will impact and assist.

The wisdom contained within these pages has existed for ages. It echoes the teachings of influential figures such as Jesus, Buddha, stoics like Marcus Aurelius, William James (the father of American Psychology), Napoleon Hill (author of "Think and Grow Rich"), and James Allen (author of "As A Man Thinketh"), among others. You will also find references to recent studies on neuroplasticity and other scientific research. However, NLP represents a mindset that explains how the mind operates to achieve what we already know it is capable of. The following quotes have withstood the test of time.

"If you can change your mind, you can change your life"

- William James, the father of American Psychology.

"A person is limited only by the thoughts that he chooses."

- James Allen, author of as a man thinketh.

"Our life is what our thoughts make it"

- Marcus Aurelius

"Be very careful about what you think. Your thoughts run your life."

- Proverbs 4:23

How powerful are your thoughts?

American surgeon Bruce Moseley conducted an experiment involving 180 patients who suffered from severe knee pain and were unresponsive to strong medication. Half of the patients underwent actual arthroscopic surgery, while the other half received only anesthetics and a small incision without the surgical procedure (placebo surgery). Astonishingly, more than half of the participants who received the placebo surgery achieved the same outcomes as those who had the real surgery. This example highlights the immense power of the mind.

Your reaction to your thoughts in a given situation can be more detrimental than the situation itself. Merely thinking negative thoughts can elevate your blood pressure and induce various anxiety levels. In fact, the chemical changes caused by negative thoughts can lead to the development of ulcers. People often ruminate over their thoughts, much like a cow chewing cud. They repeatedly bring up past events in their minds, reliving them. Even worse, they might imagine negative outcomes repeatedly despite these outcomes not having occurred yet.

Conversely, when we entertain happy thoughts and experience joy, our brain's neuroplasticity, the ability to form and reorganize synaptic connections, is positively influenced, particularly activating the prefrontal cortex. As a result, chemical reactions occur, cortisol levels decrease, and the brain responds to positive emotions by producing serotonin. Balanced serotonin levels generate feelings of calmness, focus, emotional stability, and happiness.

If we're honest with ourselves, many individuals engage in repetitive behaviors and thinking patterns year after year throughout their lives. Unconsciously, we cling to these habits because the neural pathways associated with them are easily triggered, leading to the same repetitive outcomes. This repetition can create an addiction to certain emotional states and outcomes.

This is just a fraction of how your thoughts can shape your future. However, despite the undeniable impact of thoughts on shaping your future, it's important to remember that you are not defined by your thoughts. When used correctly, these thoughts become tools with limitless potential to create your desired future.

Knowing this, consider the possibilities when you apply this knowledge to shape the future you envision.

Who controls your thoughts?

You do!

Who creates your future?

You do!

So let's begin....

Have you ever come across these falsehoods? Let's address them for what they truly are- lies.

- The myth of distinct taste regions on your tongue
- The belief that the Great Wall of China is visible from space
- The misconception that bats are blind
- The notion that sugar makes you hyper
- The story that Van Gogh severed his ear for a lover
- The misconception that we only use 10 percent of our brain
- The notion that it takes 21 days to break a habit

Wait, those are lies?

Yes, indeed. Why did you believe them? At some point, you encountered each of these lies and heard them repeatedly. You may have even found evidence that seemingly supported these lies, possibly from a different source presenting them as facts. The more you heard them, the more you believed them. Don't believe me? Go to www.destinyrising.net/truth and find the answers there.

Have you ever found yourself discussing a famous actor or singer with someone, only to have that person say, "Yeah, it's so sad they died?" Then, later, you discover that they are very much alive. Why did you believe the false information?

On November 21, 2020, an MSNBC report erroneously claimed that Bob Dylan had died in 2019 while he was in fact still alive and well.

In March 2006, a fake press release spread the news that Will Ferrell had died in a paragliding accident in southern California. However, Will Ferrell continues to make us laugh and star in movies to this day, as of the writing of this book.

In March 2011, rumors circulated on social networking sites and various news reports claimed that Jackie Chan had died from a heart attack. Jackie Chan, however, is still actively pursuing his career.

In 2005, three years before Steve Jobs passed in 2008, Bloomberg mistakenly reported his death.

Sadly, Betty White did pass away in 2021. However, false reports of her death had circulated multiple times in the years prior.

Have you encountered these lies?

- I am not good enough.
- I am not smart enough.
- I will never be able to do it.
- I don't have enough experience.

When something is repeated enough, people tend to believe it, even if it is untrue. The lies above represent just a fraction of the illusory obstacles known as limiting beliefs holding individuals back. Chapter 10 will delve deeper into breaking free from such limiting beliefs.

Only a handful of factors truly hinder people in life. However, if you pay close attention to what many people say, you will often hear them blaming their family, bad luck, or lack of education for holding them back. Some attribute their challenging upbringing or financial struggles to being held back.

Humans are the only species on this planet with unlimited potential, yet we confine and limit ourselves through our own choices. We dwell within a prison that lacks doors, windows, and bars; an internal prison. In the 1999 cult classic film The Matrix, Morpheus says to Neo, "Like everyone else, you were born into bondage; into a prison that you cannot taste or see or touch—a prison for your mind."

We often perceive numerous obstacles in our lives, but what if these obstacles are merely illusions? What if you possessed the knowledge and ability to overcome these illusory obstacles and fulfill your purpose? I consider myself a "freedom finder" dedicated to helping people transform their thinking, explore untapped resources, and discover unexplored possibilities. I aim to bring mindful awareness to your potential and open new realms of success and empowerment, liberating you from self-imposed prisons.

Some may argue, "Well, if I am content with my limitations, then why does it matter? They only affect me." but is that truly the case, or is it another lie?

I firmly believe that everyone, including you, possesses unlimited potential and has something remarkable to contribute to the world. Within you lies a unique talent, a special skill, profound knowledge, a product, or a business idea that can impact your community or even the world. However, by accepting limitations, you limit yourself and deny others the benefits of what you have to offer when you embrace and fight for your limitations.

In reality, only a few obstacles prevent people from achieving their desired outcomes, preventing them from fully engaging and living to their fullest potential. These obstacles hinder us from living with genuine passion and love and embracing life wholeheartedly.

Here are the obstacle illusions:

- Living passively (instead of taking ownership of our lives)
- Unresolved and unresourceful emotions
- Limiting beliefs and decisions
- Unnecessary attachments to people, things, emotions, the past, or control
- Internal conflicts
- Fear

To each individual, these obstacles feel incredibly real. They seem insurmountable. However, the truth is that most of them are illusions created by our own thoughts. Have you ever noticed how you can create real problems in your life through your thoughts? Our thoughts possess incredible power. Moving forward, it is crucial to recognize that these obstacle illusions are products of the immense power of our minds.

B.B.A.A.L.L. and Intention

Around two years ago, I began practicing yoga, and I discovered that many aspects of the practice extend beyond the boundaries of the yoga studio and into daily life. During one of my yoga sessions, an instructor shared a quote that resonated with me.

"A Sankalpa is like an arrow that we place in the bow of the mind. The more skillfully crafted the arrow, the more completely our actions align with it and the more accurately it approaches its target."

- Jeremy Wolf

At the start of each yoga class, my instructor encourages us to establish an intention for our practice. This particular aspect of the practice holds a significant impact as it transcends the boundaries of the yoga mat. After the class concludes, our minds continue to shape our actions and thoughts, maintaining awareness of the intention we set and carrying it into all aspects of our lives.

An intention should not be something one feels obligated to do or something that one "must," "has to," or "should" do. Rather, setting an intention should be a deeply personal and natural process that arises from our subconscious thoughts. In Sanskrit, the word for intention is Sankalpa. "san" refers to connecting with our highest truth, while "kalpa" means vow. Therefore, a Sankalpa is a vow or resolution to uphold and support our highest truth.

Now is an opportune moment for us to set an intention for reading this book, and we will do so using B.B.A.A.L.L.

This is a process I have developed to assist clients in gaining a clear vision of their desired destination and what they aim to achieve in life. I have refined it over the past few years to make it more concise and impactful. Think of it as a life audit. We will utilize the insights you gain from this exercise to set an intention for your future progress.

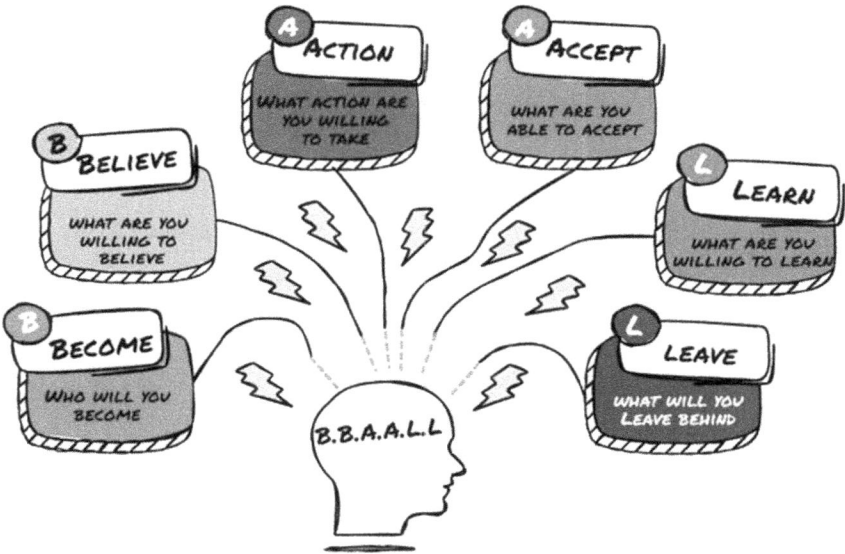

Take a moment to answer these questions, record them in a journal or notebook, or download the worksheet from www.destinyrising.net.

Ask yourself to overcome my obstacles and achieve my dreams...

1. Who am I willing to become?

We will delve into the significance of identity in more depth later in this book. For now, contemplate who you are willing to become to live the life of your dreams. Changing the words we use to describe ourselves after "I am _____" and "I am not _____" profoundly impacts our identity and mindset. The results of reshaping our identity have a ripple effect in all areas of our lives.

2.   What am I willing to believe?

Are you ready to believe in yourself? Are you willing to believe you are good enough, smart enough, and possess all the resources necessary to design a future of freedom?

3.   What action am I willing to take?

Action lies at the core of all success. Many people find themselves stuck in undesirable situations, whether a job they dislike, a toxic relationship, or a stagnant career, due to their actions or lack thereof. When we have goals, taking action and working towards them becomes paramount. For example, finding a new job entails submitting applications, making phone calls, and networking with potential employers. Action is the key to driving change. It demonstrates our willingness to do what it takes to reach our desired destination. To accomplish our goals and become the person we aspire to be, we must prove to ourselves that we are willing to put in the necessary effort. Whether starting a business or committing to a fitness routine, taking action is crucial to achieving our goals. What actions are you willing to take to reach your desired destination?

4.   What am I willing to accept?

This involves surrender and not giving up. It means accepting your current circumstances. Accepting where you are now is vital for determining the direction you want to take and embarking on the path to creating your ideal life. Have you experienced loss? Are you starting over financially? Have you attained the desired level of education? Do you have a physical disability? Accepting your current position is essential to charting the course you wish to follow. We will explore acceptance further in Chapter 6.

5.   What am I willing to learn?

Are you open to acquiring new skills, knowledge, or certifications to create effective change within yourself and others? Are you willing to learn what is necessary to establish a new business? Are you receptive to life experiences providing feedback and insights to propel you forward?

6.   What will I leave behind?

When I refer to leaving behind, I mean it in two aspects:

First, what limitations are you willing to shed? Are you prepared to leave behind limiting beliefs and decisions? Are you ready to release unresolved and unresourceful emotions? Are you willing to let go of fighting for your limitations?

Next, what legacy are you willing to leave behind? What story will people tell about you when you are no longer on this planet? What memories will you leave them with?

Notice how, in all the previous discussions, I have asked, "Are you willing?" there is a significant distinction between willingness and mere desire. While everyone has the ability, only some are truly willing. Are you willing to approach this journey with an open mind and dedicate the effort required to discover a life without limits? Are you ready to embrace a life of freedom and abundance?

Consider the qualities or virtues that you hold in high regard. Keep them in mind as you continue reading.

In the context of yoga, for instance, the qualities one may choose as their intention could include peacefulness, awareness (of the present moment, breath, love), grace, forgiveness, patience, surrender, gratitude, openness to receiving, freedom, or inner strength. These examples provide a starting point for your own contemplation.

For your intention in reading this book, review your B.B.A.A.L.L. list and tune into your inner feelings about it. What resonates with you? Hold that intention in your heart and allow it to guide you. This isn't about achieving quantifiable external outcomes but expanding your intention from within. You are a complete individual, and who you are internally reflects in all aspects of your life— your personal life, business endeavors, relationships, and projects.

Throughout this journey, your mind will quiet down, allowing you to truly discover who you are and what you genuinely desire. You will continue on your path toward becoming the thriving, creative individual you focus on. Your days will take on a deeper sense of purpose, and you will attract possibilities into your life that you never dreamed were possible.

Suppose you aspire to achieve something significant in life, transcend mediocrity, find freedom, live your passion, operate at 100%, and move beyond limitations and disempowerment. In that case, this journey is meant for you.

If you are willing, I will serve as your virtual sherpa. Together, we will embark on this journey.

I hold a profound appreciation for wine. It partially stems from how metaphorical wine is in relation to life and our purpose. However, before we delve further into overcoming your obstacle illusions, allow me to elaborate on the metaphor of wine.

You see, wine is a remarkable metaphor for our lives. Grapevines that grow in excessively fertile soil may yield abundant fruit but lack quality. On the other hand, vines that endure the challenges of rough, rocky soil often produce the highest-quality fruit. Where these vines grow shapes their character. The French refer to this as "terroir" (té·rwar), which encompasses everything that defines a vine, including its surroundings—soil, wind, rain, sun, and the vineyard's orientation towards the sun.

Life is like a bottle of wine. We have our unique growth environments. We face struggles in certain environments; these challenges often make us more resilient, determined, and experienced. However, ultimately, the purpose of wine is to be consumed. It may be crafted by the finest winemakers, sourced from the most renowned vineyards, and aged in cellars for decades. But until it is consumed, it has not fulfilled its purpose. It can be held back in cellars or bottles, which is often necessary to develop greater character and complexity.

Have you felt held back? We all have. Remember this:

You are exactly where you are meant to be at this moment in your life, developing as needed to progress to the next step.

Are you ready to fulfill your purpose?

Are you prepared to see through your obstacle illusions?

Problem, Not Problem

Every problem we have in our lives is experienced in our thoughts. For example, take a look at the illustration on the below:

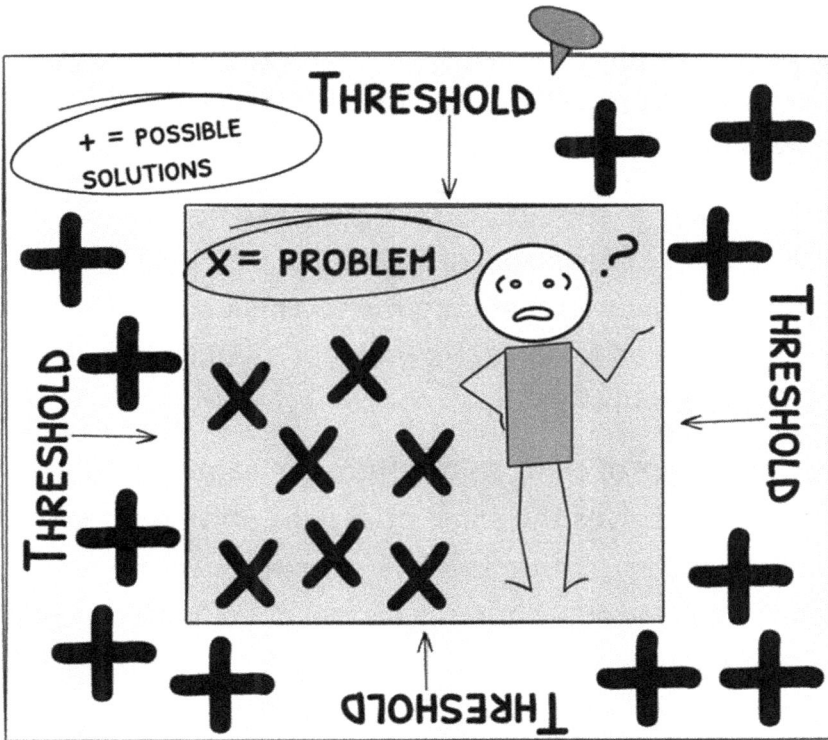

I explain this concept to my clients using the following analogy:

Imagine that we all live inside a box, and within this box are our "problems and obstacles." now, picture the box with mirrored walls, ceilings, and floors, like a house of mirrors. When we look inside the box, we see our problems and obstacles reflected on us. But what exists outside of what we can see?

Here's where it may sound strange at first, but bear with me. Outside the box, we have "not a problem." If something is not a problem, then what else could it be? Although we refer to it as a "possible solution," we often cannot see beyond our box, leading us to block potential solutions for ourselves due to the limitations we mentioned earlier.

Albert Einstein once said, "No problem can be solved from the same level of consciousness that created it." take a moment to reflect on that statement. Think about the last problem you tried to solve. How did it go? Did you quickly and effortlessly find a solution or struggle for a while?

Sometimes, approaching things from the same perspective and asking ourselves the same questions only creates a loop. By changing our perspective, gaining new knowledge, or simply talking things out, we can resonate with different ideas and change our outcomes. Other times, it takes someone outside of ourselves to expand our thinking and provide new perspectives.

Even as a coach who trains others to become certified coaches and NLP practitioners, I personally have a success coach. You might wonder why. Well, my success coach is also a Master Practitioner of NLP and possesses a wealth of techniques, knowledge, and experiences that can break through my mental models and help me achieve my desired outcomes faster than I could on my own. He often offers guidance and resources I may not have considered while troubleshooting my challenges. While these techniques are the same techniques I teach others to use as they guide their clients, the remarkable thing is that when it comes from someone else and is executed effectively, it opens new perspectives and ways of thinking, allowing us to cross a threshold. It is at that point that shifts happen. It is where problems are solved, and people experience a powerful change. The most rewarding experience is helping others create change in their own lives.

LIES AND OBSTACLE ILLUSIONS
CREATION AND REALITY

Creation

You can shape your future through the thoughts you choose, the language you use, the decisions you make, and the actions you take. Ralph Waldo Emerson once famously said, "The ancestor to every action is a thought," which holds true. Likewise, behind every action, there is a thought and a decision. So let's explore the high-level strategy that shapes your life:

Language (filtered) > Thoughts (filtered) > Decision > Action

Understanding that your current beliefs create your future is crucial because they shape the thoughts that will ultimately become your decisions and actions. Every problem or obstacle you encounter originates in your mind, and your thoughts determine whether it becomes an obstacle or not. The excellent news is that all the solutions are also within your mind. Just as your past and perceived obstacles reside in your thoughts, so does your perceived future. However, it's important to recognize that the past has already happened and cannot be changed, while the future is yet to happen. Can you see, touch, or feel your past? How about your future? Your past is merely an illusion—a collection of interpretations of past events that entered your mind.

Similarly, your future is an illusion—a prediction based on past experiences. So, where do real change and action occur? It takes place in the physical plane, in the present moment. It is not about the obstacle itself but about you becoming the solution.

I firmly believe that there are no unresourceful people, only unresourceful states. Everyone possesses the inner resources needed to succeed and achieve their desired outcomes. Sometimes, these resources lie hidden, like an unpolished gem, waiting to be revealed to help you assume a new identity—a resourceful, positive identity.

Overcoming obstacles and creating your future cannot rely on something or someone external to you. Blaming external circumstances for your future would be akin to blaming traffic lights and stop signs for your vehicle's worn-out brakes on your way to work. Clearly, the problem lies in the lack of proper maintenance. Similarly, overcoming obstacles comes from within you. While external sources may influence you, the actual change—the action—comes from within you.

Reality

A famous saying goes, "the map is not the territory." this means that everyone has their own unique "map" or model of the world. We constantly filter, generalize, and distort the information that comes into our minds. As a result, our brains shape our perception of the world, but this perception is highly inaccurate because it is based on our individual maps.

It's important to understand that our thoughts and words are not the actual events or items they represent. Our memories, thoughts, decisions, and actions are based on our perception of reality, not absolute reality.

Consider the incredible amount of information that comes in through our five senses every moment. Our eyes receive visual data, our ears receive auditory input, our nose detects smells, we have tactile sensations, and our taste buds allow us to taste flavors. Depending on the research you read, we take in anywhere from 6 to 11 million bits of information per second. However, as human beings, we are limited in our processing capabilities. We can only consciously process up to 128 bits of that information at any given time. This filter acts like an information speed limit for the traffic of information that we can attend to simultaneously.

For example, we need to process approximately 60 bits of information per second to understand what someone is saying to us. However, our brain's processing limit is only 128 bits per second. This means that with other information coming in, it becomes almost impossible for us to follow a conversation when multiple people are speaking simultaneously. It's akin to processing just one word out of every 200 books we read. Yet, this limited amount of information shapes our individual worlds. It's truly fascinating, don't you think?

Furthermore, our brains constantly monitor the environment and determine what deserves our focus and attention. This can include digital distractions like social media updates, emails, texts, news, TV shows, etc. These things compete for our brain's resources alongside important considerations like what we'll have for dinner, weekend plans, and larger concerns such as issues with friends or coworkers.

Psychologist George Miller's paper, "The Magical Number Seven, Plus or Minus Two," published in 1956, suggested that the human mind can only focus on 5-9 chunks of information at a time. More recent research indicates that most of us can handle even fewer chunks than that. Studies reveal that our conscious short-term memory can only hold 3-4 chunks of information. A chunk represents a single thought, a summarized situation, an overheard conversation, or an item on a to-do list. For example, if I wake up in the morning and think, "I need to shower, brew coffee, make the bed, and revise my presentation before today's meeting," these four chunks of information will be in my consciousness. Since science has shown that we can only process 3-4 chunks of information at a time, it's easy to understand why I might forget my laptop on the way out the door.

Filters

You may have driven by 10 fast food restaurants today and not noticed any of them, the signs they may have had out front, or the pictures of the food on the signs or windows. You may have been extremely aware if you were hungry when you drove by. However, if you weren't hungry, you may not have noticed them.

To process the enormous amount of information coming in, our brains have to filter it by deleting, distorting, and generalizing information. If they didn't, our brains would overload, and our bodies would react accordingly. As a result, some might even feel like they are losing their sanity.

Deletion

Sometimes we don't notice things, especially if we're not interested. Most of the information that we delete may be irrelevant. However, sometimes we delete information that would have been helpful if we had noticed it. Our minds delete things they know they will not use, like all the fast-food restaurants you pass while driving, all the trees you drive by, or the sound of the air conditioner running. That information did enter your mind, but your mind deleted it to make room for useful and pertinent information.

Distortion

Another way our brains sort through information is through distortion. Distortion occurs when our minds often add, subtract, or change things to make sense of them.

Have you ever seen a rope out of the corner of your eye and jumped because you thought it was a snake? This is a great example of distortion.

We also distort our reality through what is called cognitive bias. There are many cognitive biases, which are just one way we distort our reality. One of the most common cognitive biases is confirmation bias. This is when we pay attention to what supports our current beliefs and downplay what doesn't support them. An example of this is stereotyping. If someone stereotypes foreigners as bad drivers and then sees a foreigner make a driving mistake, they may say to themselves, "Just like I always say, foreigners can't drive."

Another example is when someone has a favorite team, and the referee calls against the team. Fans of the benefiting team will say it was a great call, while fans of the team it harmed will say it was a terrible call. Both sides will provide reasons to support their views, even quoting the game's rules. Another cognitive bias is social proof, where we are likely to like or believe something or buy something because many others do. The problem with cognitive biases is that they can cause us to make decisions based on personal experience and preferences rather than on the actual evidence, limiting our decision-making and keeping us inside a box.

Generalization

Generalization is the process of drawing global conclusions based on past experiences. This can be beneficial if we use the information to learn from and make broad conclusions about the world. However, it can also put people or experiences in a box and limit them. For example, someone with a bad airplane flight experience may generalize that all flights are uncomfortable. Someone who has had a couple of bad relationships may generalize that all men are jerks. Generalization can be harmful if we take a single event or a few events and make them define our entire life experience.

This can also be very powerful in a positive way. For example:

On the next page is an example of how your mind works to use deletion, distortion, and generalization:

Read the following sentence:

F1GUR471V3LY 5P34K1NG?

U C4N R34D 7H15.

7H15 M3554G3 53RV35 70 PROV3 H0W 0UR

M1ND5 C4N

D0 4M4Z1NG 7H1NG5! 1MPR3551V3 7H1NG5!

1N 7H3 B3G1NN1NG 17 WA5 H4RD BU7

N0W. 0N 7H15 LIN3 Y0UR M1ND 15

R34D1NG 17 4U70M471C4LLY

W17H 0U7 3V3N 7H1NK1NG 4B0U7 17

Technically, you should not be able to read this since there are no actual words. Even the words with the letter "o" like "how" have a zero in them. How are you able to read it?

Your mind automatically checks information from the outside world against the information on your world map. Whenever something doesn't match your world model, you adapt by referring to the model in your mind, not the actual data coming in.

This is an extremely efficient process as it allows you to quickly process information, even if it is distorted, without analyzing the data and guessing its meaning.

Not Your Map

What you experience is never a reality. Your brain constantly filters information, which has already been filtered by the time you become aware of what you're experiencing. Your "reality" is subject to your filters' deletions, distortions, and generalizations. This perceived "reality" shapes and becomes your model of the world.

We all have different maps of our individual worlds. You have your own internal map that guides the choices you make. Because your map differs from everyone else's, other people's choices and actions may not make sense to you.

People's actions and thoughts make sense from their perspective. Unfortunately, others may never fully know or understand this perspective. Often, people's actions may appear crazy or wrong when examined through your world map. This is why it is important not to judge other people's maps because if you believe that everyone should see the world the way you do, you will often be disappointed. Since we all view the world differently, no single perspective is more "real" or "true" than any other.

Imagine how much we mishear and misinterpret. For example, if we are listening to a speech, contemplating an idea, or conversing with a friend, how well are we gathering and accurately processing every piece of information? It would depend on how many other things are competing for our attention at that moment and what other thoughts we have as that information is coming in. Given this perspective, it becomes evident how easily we can be manipulated in terms of the beliefs we hold if we are not taking in and processing information as the other person expects us to hear it.

Stay On Your Mat

Let's take a moment to reflect on yoga. Yoga offers valuable insights that can be applied to life. One important lesson is to "stay on your mat." In yoga, the focus is solely on what is happening on your mat. There's no expectation or norm to pay attention to the person next to you, in front of you, behind you, or on your right or left. Each student is on their own unique path, even though they may be on a similar journey. Some may possess more skills, while others may be less experienced. Some might be practicing pose variations based on their needs and goals. People come from different backgrounds with different strengths and limitations. Instructors may have diverse training and teaching styles, incorporating various forms and disciplines of yoga. When you enter a yoga class, you must leave behind any preconceived notions and embrace a mindset of openness to learning something new.

The beauty of yoga lies in the continuous improvement of your practice. With each session, you gain more skill, knowledge, and discipline. There will be days when you effortlessly master a pose and other days when you struggle with a simple balancing pose that you usually conquer with ease. Yet, through it all, you cultivate self-compassion and refrain from judgment. Instead of competing against others or yourself, the focus is on being the best version of yourself on that particular day. This approach fosters a constructive way of living.

Acknowledging that others also shape their lives through their thoughts, language, decisions, and actions is important. While you open your mind to these new ways of thinking, you must recognize that your friends, family, and coworkers may not be on the same page yet. However, it is important to just stay on your mat; stay on *your* journey. By staying on your own mat and focusing on your personal journey, you create a space for personal growth and understanding.

Before we move on to the next chapter, I would just like to leave you with the following thought:

NOw th47 yOu knOw wh47 yOur m1nd 15 c4p4bl3 Of,

17'5 pr377y 4m4z1ng t0 th1nk 4b0u7

4ll th3 4m4z1ng 7h1ng5 yOu c4n dO.

YOur br41n 15 4 cr3471v3 4nd 1nn0v471v3 pOw3rhOus3

w17h 4 wOrld Of 3ndl3ss pO551b1l1t13s.

 W17h th15 n3wfOund und3rs74nd1ng,

 p1c7ur3 4ll th3 1ncr3d1bl3 4ch13v3m3n75 w4171ng fOr yOu 1n th3 fu7ur3.

 G3t 3xc173d 4b0u7 th3 un74pp3d p073n714l yOu h4v3 1ns1d3,

4nd g3t r34dy 70 4ccOmpl15h sOm3 s3r10us1y sp3c74cul4r 7h1ngs!

LIVING AT CAUSE

Where you currently find yourself in life is the culmination of all the decisions and indecisions you have made up to this point. This holds true for nearly everyone, with very few exceptions.

Living at cause is the secret to success in any area of life. Applying this principle to everything you undertake is a very good indication of achieving a high level of success. Many successful individuals operate under this principle without even realizing it (unconscious competence), and it serves as the driving force behind their accomplishments. This principle is known as Cause and Effect.

According to this principle, every effect, or result, is linked to a related cause. Whenever you take action or choose not to take action (remember, not taking action is still a decision), your actions or inactions will have a corresponding result.

To illustrate this, let's consider Trish's situation. Trish was running late for work, which had already happened twice that month, posing a significant disruption to operations as she relieved other shift workers. She hurriedly got into her car and noticed a low fuel notification. Looking at the gas gauge, she saw it was empty. Her husband had borrowed the car the previous evening and neglected to refuel it. Trish thought she could make it because she had 10 miles to empty. Ignoring a gas station about 2 miles away, she believed she could refuel on her way back. However, just a mile further down the road, the car notified her of one mile to empty. Soon after, the car jolted, sputtered, and ultimately shut off. Trish had run out of gas. She called her workplace to inform them of the situation, and roadside assistance arrived 45 minutes later. She eventually made it to work and her coworker had to stay late to cover her shift, resulting in frustration. At the end of her shift, Trish's supervisor called her in and informed her that she was terminated.

Naturally, Trish felt furious. She questioned her supervisor's lack of sympathy and wondered why the car's onboard computer had displayed incorrect information. She also blamed her husband for leaving the car without gas.

The important question arises: Is Trish the cause of her termination?

Was this situation completely out of Trish's control? Was there truly nothing she could have done to arrive at work on time that day? Was it the first instance of her being late to work due to unforeseen circumstances? It would be disheartening if the truth were that she was completely helpless in achieving the desired result of being on time and keeping her job.

Trish had the power to be at Cause for the problems that arose. There were actions she could have taken. For instance, Trish could have ensured there was enough gas in the car even before her husband used it for errands. She could have left the house with ample time to stop for gas on her way to work and then to the gas station afterward. Trish could have also been punctual the other days. Isn't it amazing that she had so many choices available to her? If she had chosen to take responsibility for any of the issues leading up to this final straw, she may not have lost her job.

Where you are in life right now is a culmination of all the decisions and indecisions you have made up to this point.

Imagine the freedom, power, and choices you would have if you lived at Cause for everything that happened in your life—the good and the bad. If you decide to be at Cause, you will suddenly notice that life offers you more choices and options to deal with all the things that come up.

Not happy with where you live? If you are living at Cause, you can find a solution. You can sell your house and move. You could move local or to another state. You can choose to rent. There are unlimited possibilities! But wait, you may say, I can't just find another job and leave my extended family to move to another state. Why not? Many people make decisions like this every day. There are numerous options available, but you must first stop finding excuses and, instead, find solutions. In fact, don't just find the solutions, be a part of the solution. Be the solution!

Effect is actually just an illusion that becomes a self-fulfilling prophecy. People who believe things happen "to them" give away their power and allow themselves to be at the mercy of external circumstances. This, too, is a choice and, therefore, an illusion. Moreover, Effect gives rise to excuses for why something happened.

While excuses reside on the side of effect, results reside on the side of "cause."

Where the victim mentality lives on the side of effect, the victor mentality lives on the side of cause.

Most people find excuses for not doing, having, or accomplishing things. The mindset often sounds like: "I can't afford it," "We don't have enough money," "I don't have enough education," "I'm too old," "I'm too young," or "I have a job that doesn't give me time to start a side business." These are examples of living in effect instead of living at cause. Most people give away their personal power and are left with only a handful of excuses and reasons for not being where they want to be in life. When you stop fighting for your limitations and start living at cause, you will begin to attain what you want in life.

For the next week, I challenge you to take on everything in your life from this new perspective. Be at cause for everything that happens in your life every time. If someone cuts you off in traffic and flips you off, decide how you will be at cause. Embrace this mindset for a week, and you will be surprised at how different you feel. Eliminate excuses and live at cause in your life! Achieve all the greatness and success that is meant for you!

This applies to every aspect of your life, from your financial status to your relationships, to your happiness and to your work. Take a moment to reflect on the areas where you want to make changes. Remember, you are at cause for everything, every time.

Start assuming you are at cause and act accordingly.

Awareness is a crucial key to change. Have you ever considered that when someone asks you a question, and you respond with "I need to think about it," you are essentially saying "I need to ask myself questions?" When you are thinking about anything, you are actually asking yourself questions. The issue is that most people tend to ask themselves disempowering questions, such as "why did I do that," "why do I always mess things up," "why do these bad things always happen to me," or "how will I leave this job, relationship, or situation?"

Asking better questions is essential for achieving better results in life.

Your mind will always seek answers to your questions and find evidence to support those questions. This is due to your reticular activating system (RAS).

Your RAS is a bundle of neurons near the top of the spinal column, about the diameter of your pinky finger, that connects to your visual, auditory, and kinesthetic senses (sight, sound, and feeling). As your brain is bombarded with information, it filters out what you don't need or what you have programmed yourself not to notice. Some information, such as threats to your safety or hearing someone call your name, bypasses this filter. When you consciously focus your awareness in a specific area, your RAS is activated and tunes into relevant information. For example, try looking around the room and noticing everything green. Now shift your focus to notice everything red. Those things were there before, but you were unaware until they entered your conscious awareness. While the task was initially to focus and be aware of green items, any red item was filtered out until your attention was called to it.

This is why it is important to have intention and live with purpose. The issue arises when we express desires or aspirations but use unresourceful phrases like "it would be nice to," "I want to", "I would like to", or "I hope to." These phrases carry a sense of doubt or presupposition of doubt, which will be addressed below.

Using purpose-filled words such as "intend" or "will" banishes doubt and activates the RAS, just like someone calling your name. It begins to sift and filter the information to help you become aware and act on your intention. Your conscious and subconscious minds become congruent, allowing you to see, hear, and understand the things that will help you achieve your intention.

Our RAS also activates when we ask ourselves questions. Disempowering questions like "why did I do that," "why do I always mess things up," "why do these bad things always happen to me," "how am I ever going to get out of this job, relationship, situation" prompt our minds to come up with answers.

The issue with disempowering questions is that they contain presuppositions. Presuppositions are assumptions you must accept as true to continue with what you are asking, saying, or thinking.

For example, the question "why do I always mess things up?" presupposes that things are always getting messed up. Similarly, "why do these bad things always happen to me?" presupposes that bad things always happen to you.

No matter the question, our RAS goes on a search for answers. Asking better questions is vital for achieving better results in life.

Here are some empowering questions to consider:

- For what purpose have I created the situation I am in?
- What positive lessons in this situation can I apply to future circumstances?
- What if _____ were possible?
- What if I could do it?
- What if there is a solution?
- What might that be, or what might the potential solutions be?
- How can I _____?
- How can I accomplish it?
- How can I create a solution?

Being at cause and having awareness are prerequisites for all change and the certainly are the foundations of creating lasting change. Eliminate excuses and live at cause in your life! Achieve all the greatness and success that is meant for you!

ATTENTION AND ENERGY

With this mindset of empowerment established, let's explore how our thoughts and attention play a crucial role someone cuts you off in traffic and you become angry, honk your horn, and feel your heart rate rise, who is at fault for those actions and your increased heart rate? Did they cause those reactions in you? Absolutely not. They had no control over you. Did they restrain you and force you to get angry? No.

This example teaches us that nothing external to us truly causes anything; it only reveals what is inside. Have you heard the metaphor, "if you squeeze an orange, what comes out?" The answer is orange juice. Why? Because that's what's inside the orange. When life squeezes you, what comes out? What emerges is what resides within you.

Like all things, external circumstances do not cause anger or frustration. Our interpretation, our perspective on what is happening, exposes what is within us. In fact, there are only three underlying causes of anger: unmet wants, expectations, or goals; feeling threatened; and using anger as a mask for other emotions. Anger may exist within us, anchored by past situations or events, and can be triggered by a new situation or event.

For example, perhaps you had an argument with your significant other before leaving the house, maybe you're facing unmet expectations or goals at work, or perhaps

46

while driving, someone cut in front of you and damaged your car, resulting in feelings of being threatened. In the future when a similar event happens, all those internal feelings and associations from the initial event flood in, and you react to those anchors and triggers. One of the few things we have control over in life is how we respond to anything that comes our way. By reacting with anger, or any other unhelpful emotion, we relinquish our personal power.

This pattern repeats in various situations. We become so immersed in the situation that we suffer within it. We may laugh, cry, or become angry. Our thoughts and emotions carry energy, and being aware of those emotions is crucial.

There is an ancient Huna principle called Makia, which means "where attention goes, energy flows." As Dr. Wayne Dyer used to say, "What you think about is what expands." Imagine chewing gum and blowing a bubble. The air inflates the gum. Similarly, our thoughts expand. When people say, "my life is good" or "my life is bad," they are referring to the pleasantness or unpleasantness of their thoughts (internal representations) and emotions. Their thoughts combine with their emotions, shaping their experiences into good or bad days, happiness or sadness in the moment, and ultimately good or bad lives overall.

People often misinterpret their thoughts and emotions as just experiencing life and react accordingly. Everyone is always told life is full of highs and lows, but how you choose to react can greatly affect your own view on each situation and let you be in control of those highs and lows.

If our thoughts carry energy and expand, and if the only internal resources we are aware of are limiting beliefs like "I'm not good enough," "I'm not smart enough," "I'll never succeed," or "I lack experience," what will happen?

That energy of limitation will expand, and we will find evidence to support those statements that are false and turn them into a reality.

If we truly understand the power of our thoughts and the energy they carry, we can embark on a journey of expansion and transformation. It all starts with recognizing and challenging those limiting beliefs that hold us back. You are more than good enough, smart enough, and capable enough to achieve anything you set your mind to! So let's kick those limiting beliefs to the curb and make room for a whole new level of success and abundance in our lives.

How do we initiate this process of change?

I am glad you asked! To initiate this process of change, we need to activate our Reticular Activating System (RAS) – that incredible internal guidance system that filters and brings our attention to what truly matters. By consciously directing our focus and heightening our awareness, we create new neural pathways and pave the way for a positive shift in our mindset. It's like shining a bright spotlight on the possibilities that exist within us, illuminating the endless resources and strengths that have been lying dormant.

 Activating our RAS brings about awareness. We create new neurochemical pathways through our heightened consciousness by consciously being aware. Our prefrontal cortex signals the rest of our nervous system that we need to deactivate automatic responses and prepare for a new process.

All living things possess a certain level of awareness. For example, trees are attuned to sunlight and water, adjusting their growth and positioning their limbs and roots accordingly. Likewise, animals anticipate the changing seasons and construct nests for their offspring. Humans, however, have the capacity for expanded awareness, although many choose to live within the confines of the plant and animal awareness.

By nature, you already possess the necessary resources to achieve success. You are a remarkable work in progress, just as you are. The key is to be open to viewing things from a fresh perspective, allowing you to uncover the inherent design and resources within you and unlock their potential.

Consider the image on the following page. What do you see?

Now take the page and put the book where you can walk back about 20 feet. The further back you walk, the clearer you can see the image of the girl. Amazing, right? When I tell you what to look for, you can see the image because the design has been revealed to you. Just like your obstacle illusions, you can make change happen once you see through them.

Imagine tackling life's hurdles as deciphering mind-bending optical illusions – a fascinating mental adventure where challenges mirror the cognitive tricks that mess with our visual perception! Picture your brain as a high-tech command center, processing signals from life's experiences to build your personal worldview. Life's obstacles, like optical illusions, play with your brain's habit of simplifying and rationalizing what it sees, sometimes leading you to interpret situations based on past experiences, creating a distorted reality.

Think of your brain as a detective on a mission, efficiently deciphering patterns. Optical illusions throw conflicting cues your way, just like life's complex situations that demand sharp problem-solving skills to uncover the truth amid the chaos.

Consider the importance of context in optical illusions – how surrounding information influences what you perceive. Life's challenges are like that; they manipulate the context of your experiences, prompting assumptions that may not align with the true situation.

Visualize your cognitive functions as a detective navigating through blind spots, filling in the gaps based on surrounding information. Life's challenges pull the same stunt, exploiting cognitive blind spots and making it tricky to see the complete picture. Just like illusions capitalize on gaps in understanding, life's hurdles often prompt us to fill in informational voids with assumptions that may lack accuracy.

Essentially, life's challenges, like optical illusions, playfully engage with your brain's knack for pattern recognition and contextual interpretation. This dynamic interplay highlights the lively and sometimes mystifying ways in which your mind constructs your reality.

Know that, similar to deciphering an optical illusion, you've got the mental resilience to navigate through life's twists and turns with discernment and clarity.

Just for fun, the following pages contain some additional images that are optical illusions.

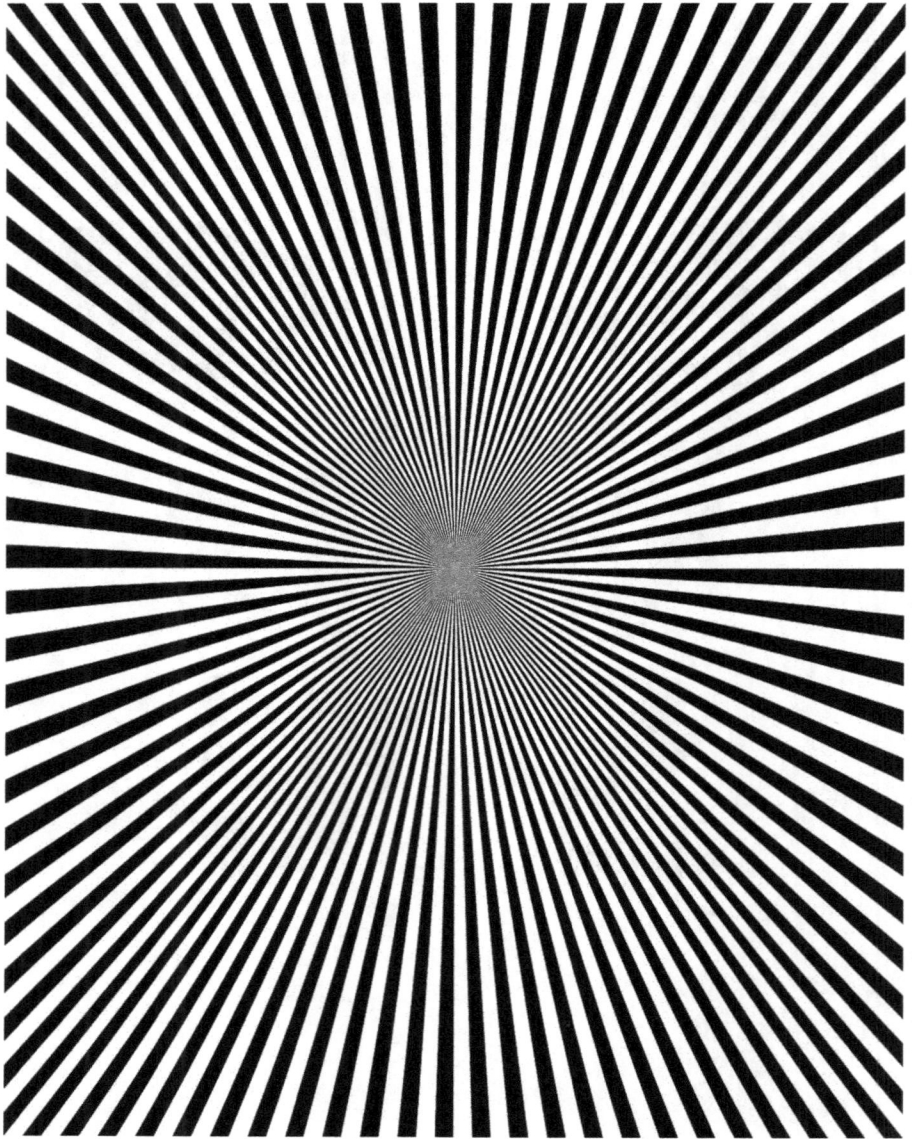

LAYERS OF THE MIND

The Conscious and Subconscious Mind

You possess one mind comprised of two parts: the conscious and unconscious. The conscious mind is aware of the present moment. It operates like a computer, continuously processing information and subjecting it to logical tests to make sense of the world. It functions as the CEO of your mental processes, making deliberate choices and decisions that are then carried out by the subconscious mind. This allows you to exert control over your actions rather than being solely driven by emotions and sensory experiences.

In contrast, the unconscious mind operates outside the realm of logic and morality. It takes a less critical approach to the information received from the conscious mind, freeing up the conscious mind to focus on other tasks such as quick decision-making and judgments. The unconscious mind handles various functions, including running and preserving the body, storing memories and emotions, and other intricate details that would otherwise overwhelm the conscious mind and impede its decision-making capabilities.

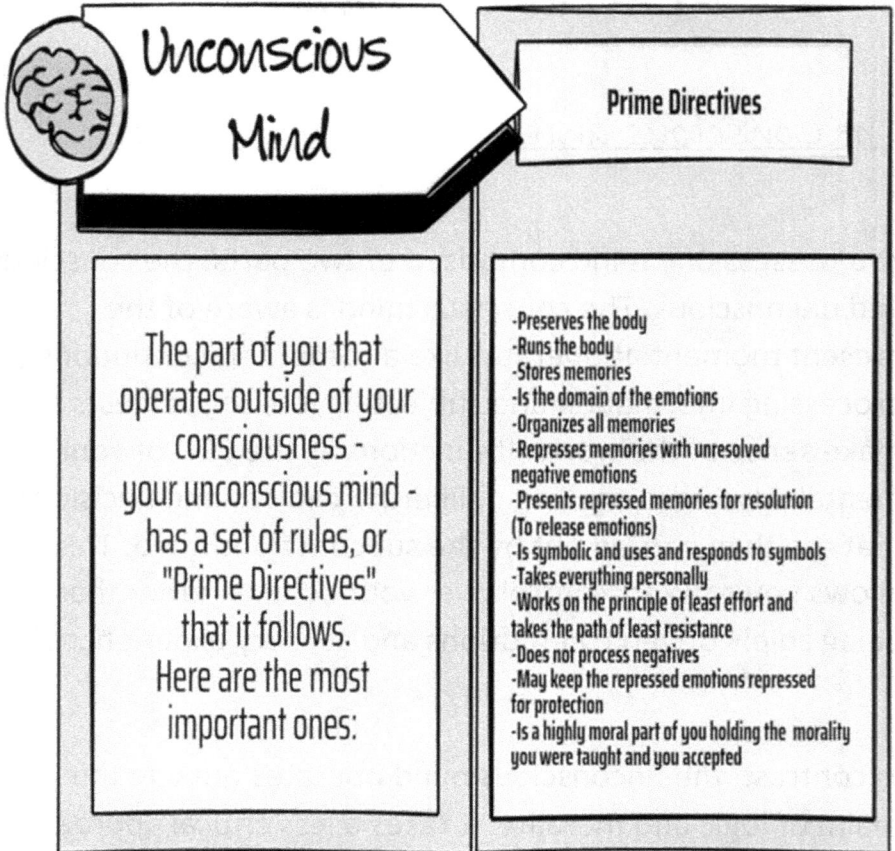

Unconscious Mind

Prime Directives

The part of you that operates outside of your consciousness - your unconscious mind - has a set of rules, or "Prime Directives" that it follows. Here are the most important ones:

-Preserves the body
-Runs the body
-Stores memories
-Is the domain of the emotions
-Organizes all memories
-Represses memories with unresolved negative emotions
-Presents repressed memories for resolution (To release emotions)
-Is symbolic and uses and responds to symbols
-Takes everything personally
-Works on the principle of least effort and takes the path of least resistance
-Does not process negatives
-May keep the repressed emotions repressed for protection
-Is a highly moral part of you holding the morality you were taught and you accepted

It can be likened to a guardian angel, safeguarding you from harm's way.

When we seek to bring about change within ourselves, society conditions us to look outside of ourselves toward our external environment. Think about the commercials you've seen on television or the social media posts that market products, all showcasing images of happy people. Whether it's a refreshing beverage, a dream vacation, an influencer promoting the latest product, a new restaurant, or a fashionable outfit, these connections to the external world form the initial layer of our conscious mind. The unconscious mind is always focused on protecting you and keeping you safe.

Refer to the following diagram to visualize each layer of the mind. This model provides a simplified understanding of the human experience and how we approach problems or change. It proposes six levels that can be used to analyze our experiences, offering profound insights.

Take a moment to examine the chart and reflect on the following questions, which will help you better understand how you perceive yourself in relation to the layers of the mind.

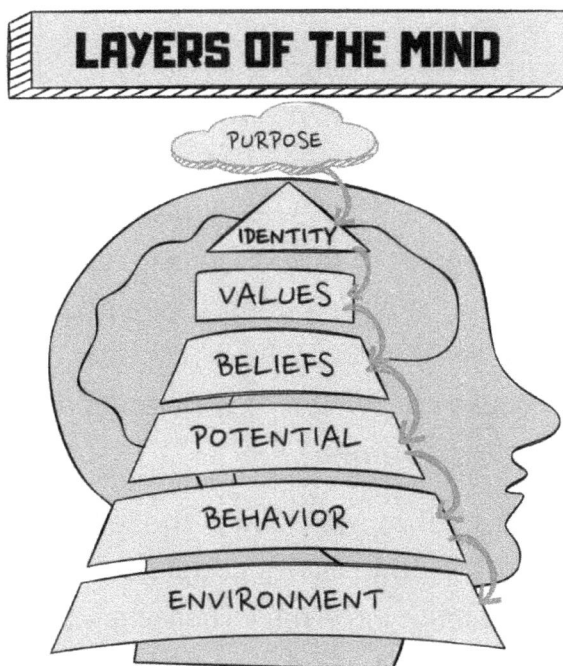

LAYERS OF THE MIND

PURPOSE

IDENTITY

VALUES

BELIEFS

POTENTIAL

BEHAVIOR

ENVIRONMENT

Do you primarily define yourself by what you do, focusing on your skills and abilities? Or do you define yourself based on your values and what truly matters to you? Is your identity centered around who you are, with character and personality at the forefront? Alternatively, do you define yourself in terms of your purpose, intention, or higher calling?

Environment

Our conscious mind is responsible for our awareness of the external world. It is the part of our mind that is most connected to the environment we consciously perceive. The foundational layer of the mind is the environment itself. When individuals seek to make a change, they often focus on this level.

The environment level encompasses our physical location, events, and the people with whom we interact. Although it raises questions like, "Where am I now?" and "what is happening around me?" this level involves recognizing the opportunities and external threats in our lives. For example, if the goal is to get in shape, joining a gym and getting a trainer might be the first steps. However, it is common to experience setbacks and return to old habits due to the familiarity of the environment.

The environment level of the mind is the least effective in creating long-term impact. Many people set goals based solely on changing their external circumstances. They aspire to have a specific amount of money, own a particular car, or buy a certain house. Similarly, individuals may continuously jump from one relationship to another without addressing the underlying patterns. In my interactions with people seeking freedom, I often observe them searching for it in new environments. One common environmental action is an individual changing jobs in hopes of finding their desired change. Solely changing environments usually leads to that person finding themselves back in their old mindset unless they make changes at other levels as well.

As we progress through the layers of the mind, we delve deeper into the subconscious mind. Moving from the environment level to the behavior level, we transition from the conscious to the subconscious mind. Each subsequent layer holds greater power than the ones before it, as changes at higher levels have a trickle-down effect. Like a chain reaction, altering one level can impact the levels below it. Since the effort required to change something at a higher level is no different from changing something at a lower level, it is wise to aim for the most significant and lasting impact. This necessitates delving deeper into the mind.

Most individuals seek change that extends beyond a short-term duration of two weeks or two months. They aspire to make lasting improvements for the rest of their lives.

Behavior

The next layer we explore is behavior, which encompasses our actions. It revolves around the question, "What am I doing?" for instance, if you want to become fit and build muscle, you change your behavior by exercising. When you alter your behavior and engage in regular exercise, you not only achieve different results but also impact your environment.

You will notice changes in your body after consistently working out over a period of time. Changing your behavior has a trickle-down effect, automatically influencing the lower levels of the mind. While some behaviors are subconscious habits, most of them are conscious choices. If you're not deeply aligned with the new behavior you're attempting to adopt, it becomes challenging to sustain it. This is why New Year's resolutions often fail to create lasting change; deeper layers of the mind must be addressed to bring about true transformation. Although behavioral changes yield results, these outcomes tend to be short-term. Now, let's delve deeper into the next level.

Potential

Potential refers to what you can achieve with the skills and knowledge you possess. It involves utilizing your capabilities to accomplish something great. While potential is influenced by what you know, it also relies on how you apply it. This is what makes potential so powerful. The question at this level is, "what knowledge do I have, and what skills do I possess?"

There is a trickle-down effect because tapping into your potential leads to specific behaviors, producing results in your environment. There are various ways to enhance your potential. One effective method is continuous learning. You can expand your potential by reading books or taking courses that expose you to new information or different ways of doing things. The newfound knowledge automatically triggers changes in your behavior without requiring conscious effort. For instance, having a personal trainer who imparts new knowledge to your workout routine positively affects your fitness goals and results in automatic behavioral change. You find yourself preparing for workouts and waking up ready for exercise without much thought.

Similarly, when you take our NLP (Neuro-Linguistic Programming) course, you will learn new language patterns for effective communication. This newfound potential naturally alters your communication style, influencing the people around you and the dynamics of your environment. It's important to note that the trickle-down effect can work in both positive and negative directions. Unlocking new potential regarding communication, for example, leads to behavior change and different outcomes. Conversely, limited potential restricts behavior and impedes progress.

You possess vast untapped potential, much of which you may not even be aware of. The key to unlocking and tapping into this potential lies in the next layer of the mind.

Beliefs

Beliefs are closely linked to values. Beliefs represent what you hold to be true about yourself, others, and the world around you. They reside in the deeper layers of the subconscious mind and profoundly impact your decision-making process. To identify your beliefs, consider the words you use after phrases like "this means" or "they are." These thought patterns can help shed light on your underlying beliefs.

For example, if you believe that "rain means a gloomy day," that reflects your belief. On the other hand, someone else may believe that "rain means a peaceful day is on the way," which demonstrates a different belief. This example highlights why the things we say and our perceptions at each level, leading up to beliefs, are so significant.

Beliefs can be incredibly empowering or limiting, and their influence is often subtle. They become deeply ingrained in our worldview, leading us to accept them as reality without recognizing them as beliefs. Have you ever believed you were not good or smart enough? When you hold such beliefs, you will find evidence supporting them everywhere you look. Our beliefs act as filters through which we interpret the world. They shape our perception of ourselves and our capabilities. Even if there is ample evidence to the contrary, we fail to see it when our beliefs are not aligned with that evidence.

The mind activates the RAS, filtering information that confirms our beliefs about ourselves. It magnifies every mistake and fuels self-criticism. This is why language and beliefs are so influential and impactful.

The trickle-down effect is immensely powerful when you release a limiting belief or adopt an empowering belief. For instance, changing beliefs about your abilities and intelligence unlocks your potential and automatically leads to behavioral changes. These new behaviors, in turn, bring about significant and enduring transformations at the environmental level. See how the trickle-down effect is put into motion?

Moreover, if you plan to train with Destiny Rising and work with clients, understanding these deeper levels of the mind will revolutionize your approach. Unlike many success coaches, therapists, and hypnotherapists who primarily focus on behavior and environment, you will guide your clients to explore and transform their beliefs. By delving deeper, you can help them overcome personal blocks and move toward achieving their goals. However, it's important to recognize that the ultimate responsibility for change lies with the clients themselves; coaches are merely guides.

We hold numerous beliefs that often operate outside of our conscious awareness. Our beliefs are shaped by various systems and programs that influence us without our realization. Only when we are intentional and aware of these layers can we create real and lasting change.

Values

Values serve as your compass, guiding you through life by helping you determine what is important and right for you. They underpin your beliefs and shape your actions. Values operate at a deep level, often outside of conscious awareness. Many people are unaware of their values and struggle to explain why they make certain choices or behave in specific ways. They may not understand these choices and behaviors are processed at the subconscious level.

Values can differ among individuals based on ethnicity, nationality, and geographic region. We can observe differences in people's approaches to life, even if we can't pinpoint the exact cause. Values dictate how we allocate our time and energy.

Consider your own habits and how they have shaped your values and beliefs. Do you consume fast food? Do you wake up early, even when unnecessary? Do you drink in moderation? Do you engage in regular exercise? Do you kiss on the first date? Do you remain faithful to your spouse? Do you eat meat? Do you give up before reaching your goals? The reasons behind these behaviors are influenced by your values.

Personal values act as the driving force behind your actions in life. If a goal aligns with your values, you will invest time and effort into achieving it. Your values provide motivation for pursuing your goals. When something is deeply important to you subconsciously, you are compelled to take action. Conversely, when you neglect to act in alignment with your values, you may experience regret or a sense of missed opportunity.

Values not only shape how you allocate your energy, they also serve as a filter through which you view your own past behaviors and the behaviors of others. We all have a values filter that unconsciously influences our judgments of others. For example, if you witness someone being rude, you may label them as a bad person. On the other hand, if you observe a husband opening a car door for his wife, you may view him as a gentleman. These assessments are based on how others align with your values and your expectations of how people should treat one another.

Values hold great power and can often lead to conflicts within individuals. When your life choices clash with your deeply held values, it can create internal turmoil that needs resolution. However, an even deeper level of the subconscious mind profoundly influences one's identity.

Identity

The layer of identity is responsible for some of the most transformative and permanent shifts in our lives. Identity emerges from "I am" or "I am not" statements we tell ourselves. Joseph Campbell said these two phrases are the most powerful in the universe because they shape your destiny. Within you, there exist multiple identities that define who you are. For instance, I identify as an entrepreneur, which influences my actions, values, beliefs, potential, and behaviors.

To delve into identity, ask yourself, "Who am I when I am engaged in this activity?" or "who do I need to be or become to achieve this?" pay close attention to the "I am" statements you make internally and in your interactions with others. Take note of the "I am" statements those around you use.

Equally impactful are the "I am not" statements. Some individuals may say, "I am not an entrepreneur." This statement limits their values, beliefs, and potential and confines them to a limited environment. While not everyone desires to be an entrepreneur, the "I am not" statement can hinder their mindset if someone envies entrepreneurial traits but fails to adopt them.

When change occurs at the level of identity, it does not require conscious effort. Many people try to change using willpower, which involves consciously defying what they truly want to do. The problem with relying solely on willpower is that our conscious mind is limited, easily distracted by other things, and can undermine our efforts. This is why willpower often falls short of our intentions, as we attempt to exert conscious control over everything, which is simply not feasible long term.

Willpower operates at the conscious levels of environment and behavior, requiring ongoing conscious thought and being susceptible to distractions and abandonment. A typical scenario is when someone says to themself, "I really need to work on my health, so I'll get up early and go to the gym. Oh, I can just snooze the alarm clock. Alright, I'll start tomorrow for sure." Willpower has lost the fight today and likely again tomorrow. This individual working on their health has not yet made being fit their identity; it is not who they believe they are.

Consider individuals who adopt the identity of being vegan or vegetarian. When someone identifies as a vegetarian, you wouldn't expect them to consume meat. That behavior goes against their identity and beliefs.

Society perpetuates the illusion that external factors can transform individuals into what they desire to be, leading to happiness. The belief is that acquiring possessions, such as a great job, a new car, or a house, will bring happiness. However, this is a profound illusion. True happiness stems not from what you possess but from what you do with your life. If you seek happiness, engage in activities that bring you joy.

One of my mentors shares a powerful saying, "As soon as you become who you want to be, then you will do the things that it takes to have what you want." This concept is about finding freedom and realizing that you don't have to wait for someone or something to transform you. You already possess the qualities and potential within you.

When I was a child, my parents gave me a BMX bike. It fascinated me, and my dad taught me how to pedal, steer, balance, and brake. Did I become a bike rider as soon as he taught me those skills? Of course not. He then shared his experience of learning to ride a bike, emphasizing that anyone can do it. He pushed me, and I attempted to ride, but I wobbled and crashed. Despite the falls, he encouraged me to keep trying. Finally, after several attempts, there was a moment when I believed I could do it and acted on that belief. At that moment, even before I could ride smoothly without crashing, I assumed the identity of "I am a bike rider" and that is when I actually became a bike rider.

The principle of "there is no failure, only feedback" applies here. How can a child fail to ride a bike? Only by giving up and quitting before they become bike riders. The feedback received through the process, such as balancing left and right or not braking too fast, allows us to adjust and make changes until we succeed.

Don't wait for external circumstances to grant you permission to be who you want. Instead, step into the mindset of someone already experiencing wealth, health, happiness, or any other quality you desire. Take action today to make it happen.

Some may argue that you can't consider yourself wealthy until you have a certain amount of money in your bank account. However, this mindset perpetuates a cycle of poverty. Wealthy individuals attract wealth, while those with a poverty mindset do not. If you aspire to be wealthy, you must shift your mindset and claim that identity for yourself.

Similar to how I became a bike rider, not when I was taught how, but when I believed I could do it and acted on that belief, start believing and acting on your desired identity. Initiate changes at the highest level, and the other levels will fall into place as you naturally begin to transform them. For example, if it initially feels overwhelming, you can start by saying, "I am an entrepreneur." Alternately, you can modify your phrasing to say, "I am becoming an entrepreneur," "I am in the process of becoming a writer," or "I am willing to believe I can be a success coach." Tailor your statements to your specific aspirations. The key is to recognize that as soon as you become who you want to be, you will naturally take the actions necessary to achieve what you desire.

Purpose

The highest layer of your mind is purpose. It represents the one thing you prioritize above all else to the extent that you would be willing to sacrifice your life. For some individuals, this could be their country or religion. Others might resonate more with a political cause, while some prioritize love, peace, or family. It's also possible to have a combination of these purposes.

When people achieve a goal, they may wonder what comes next or how they should feel. They might ask, "is this all there is?" This feeling of being lost stems from a lack of purpose. Maintaining motivation and moving forward can be challenging without a sense of purpose. That's why focusing on things beyond your immediate obstacles is important.

Living with intention based on your purpose is crucial. Remember our discussion of Sankalpa in Chapter 1? You need to know the purpose behind your actions and decisions and then carry them out intentionally. Asking yourself, "for what purpose?" is a powerful question. You can also inquire, "what am I a part of that is beyond myself?" or "what is more important to me than I am to myself?"

When you think, "I really want to find a new job, lose weight, start a business, find a partner," or any other desire, it's essential to ask, "for what purpose?" Once you have the answer, continue asking the same question for each subsequent response. This is commonly referred to as understanding the "why." However, I suggest replacing the disempowering question "why" with the more empowering question "For what purpose?" or "What is important to me about this?" These questions help clarify your purpose and define what an empowering life means to you when you prioritize your values.

THE ILLUSION OF LABELS

I believe what many people ultimately desire in life revolves around abundance and freedom. While these aspirations may differ for everyone, based on my experience as a coach, these two outcomes are often sought after. Some individuals may desire to be their own boss or accumulate a certain amount of wealth, such as a million or two million dollars. I however, believe these desires ultimately boil down to a longing for abundance and freedom.

Financial freedom entails doing what you want, when and where you want to do it, with whomever you choose. On the other hand, true freedom, which I refer to as mental freedom, involves living life on your own terms and not being constrained by the belief that things must be done a certain way simply because they've always been done that way. To attain true freedom, it is important to detach yourself from the emotions, labels, and standards you acquired during your upbringing. Labels are illusory constructs. It's important to remember that language is manmade, and objects don't come into the world with pre-assigned names. People often assign labels to individuals and things, expecting them to conform to certain expectations based on those labels. You can act beyond their limitations by not giving power to these labels.

For instance, let's consider Keri, a talented volleyball player regarded as the top athlete in her school. Due to her commitment to volleyball practice and participation in club-level volleyball, she was never invited to engage in activities like playing miniature golf or going on weekend trips to amusement parks with her classmates. She was labeled as "the athlete." People often use labels to define others, but in doing so, they limit the person's ability to exist beyond those expectations. It's likely that you have also been assigned labels at some point in your life. Perhaps you were called the class clown. Although you may have enjoyed that label, it may have come with certain expectations that made it difficult for you to embrace and enjoy other roles, such as being seen as intelligent, athletic, or creative.

Frequently, people assign labels to others or things to feel better about themselves or to justify their dislike for someone or something. However, in doing so, they close themselves off from truly getting to know the person. Labels are not inherently negative, but we should be mindful of how they influence our perception of ourselves and others. By detaching from labels, you allow yourself the freedom to act outside the confines of those expectations and take back the power from the label, empowering yourself.

I recently had a conversation with a retired executive who has ample financial resources. He expressed that if he could go back in time, he would make only three changes that he neglected due to being too preoccupied with work:

- He would prioritize physical fitness and care for his body. He now realizes the importance of daily stretching and can touch his toes for the first time since retiring.

- He would have traveled more.
- He would have spent more time with his family.

Despite having financial abundance, he did not possess true freedom. Freedom is the ultimate desire for most of us.

When I discuss abundance and prosperity, it extends beyond mere monetary wealth. While money can be a measure of abundance, there is much more to it. Abundance and prosperity encompass having positive aspects in your life that hold personal significance. This could include good health, fulfilling relationships, a satisfying career, or anything else that brings you joy. To cultivate greater abundance and prosperity, reflect on what would genuinely make you happy while recognizing that some people possess substantial wealth yet feel deeply lonely. Abundance encompasses more than money; it encompasses what brings you happiness. Through my interactions with clients, they have expressed that their true sources of happiness are abundant love, nurturing relationships, well-being, and travel experiences, among other things. What brings you happiness? What is your resource you have been given to fulfill your mission in life?

With identity explored, let's examine another obstacle illusion - internal conflicts.

INTERNAL CONFLICTS

Tonya gazed out the window, her mind flooded with memories of the past seven years. She had joined the company she worked for right out of college, thrilled at the opportunity. In the beginning, she formed close bonds with her colleagues Mia, Sanjay and Maddie as they were all newcomers learning the ropes together. Over time, they shared the workload on big campaigns, celebrated wins for clients, and consoled each other when projects fell through.

While Tonya felt a draw towards the idea of pursuing a new career in a field aligned with her values, she hesitated to leave her friends and break up the dream team they had formed. She and Mia even created a morning ritual of coffee together before tackling their overflowing inboxes. Could she abandon her team when they had relied on her skills for so long?

Beyond colleagues, Tonya also felt immense loyalty to her company's mission of promoting ethical companies making positive social change. She had loved working with these clients over the years.

Finally, the steady paycheck and matching 401K her company provided for Tonya's years of service made walking away even harder. She had been securely building savings, with plans to buy a condo in the next year or two. The risk of launching a new consulting business felt destined to delay everything she had financially worked towards.

Weighing it all, Tonya put her head in hands, the complexity of choosing between security and purpose making her decision excruciatingly impossible. She wished the various forces of loyalty tugging her in opposite directions would just resolve themselves.

Janice sighed in frustration and confessed, "I need to cut down on my chocolate consumption. Part of me understands that I should reduce it, but another part of me doesn't want to give it up!"

Janice had always had a sweet tooth, but over the last year her chocolate cravings had become extreme and unrelenting. After a long day at the accounting office, poring over endless spreadsheets, her mind would fixate on the chocolate she kept stashed in her desk drawer. No matter how much she ate, one or two overtly rich chocolate bars per night didn't seem to satisfy her.

In the mornings, Janice would vow to reduce her chocolate intake, yet by the time mid-afternoon fatigue and stress set in, she'd be wandering past the vending machine or corner store seeking that molten cocoa rush. Though she hated feeling like a slave to such an obsessive habit, the temporary bliss as the chocolate melted across her tongue made the lack of self-control worth it. Or so she continued telling herself despite feeling increasingly trapped in this cycle.

Janice felt two sides waging a fierce battle within her around the chocolate addiction. On one side, her intuitive inner Wisdom knew consuming large quantities of sugary chocolate bars ran counter to her health goals and getting enough proper whole foods. Wisdom was aware that balanced nutrition and restorative self-care would better serve reducing Janice's daily stress.

However, Wisdom's vision was continually overridden by Janice's Craving - an inner saboteur part that hijacked any willpower once fixated on chocolate. Craving whispered justifications about needing comfort rewards after draining workdays. It carelessly dismissed any negative impacts too much chocolate might have. Ultimately Craving manipulated Janice's behavior against her own intentions.

Can you relate to either of these situations or something similar? Whether it is relationships, addictions, grief, or career, many of us have experienced the feeling of being pulled in different directions. It's as if one part of us wants to pursue one course of action while another wants something entirely different. It's like a mental tug of war. Some coaches call this the conflict between the adult and child parts of ourselves, the left and right brains, or even the mind and heart. Most of the time, we can resolve these conflicts and move forward. There are instances when resolving that internal conflict becomes more challenging.

Integrating these "parts" within ourselves creates harmony and alignment within our unconscious mind. This integration leads to greater congruence, empowerment, and clarity in decision-making and actions. When our values align with the functioning of our subconscious mind, we experience a profound shift.

Parts integration is an effective NLP technique specifically designed to resolve internal conflicts. We teach this technique in our NLP practitioner certification course. It is known for its powerful impact in helping individuals find resolution and achieve personal growth.

Parts integration grew out of NLP's early roots in modeling human excellence and understanding subjective experience. Co-founders Richard Bandler and John Grinder researched exceptional therapists like Fritz Perls who facilitated inner communication between conflicting "parts" of a client's psyche.

Bandler and Grinder began codifying techniques, creating a way to map and personify the inner forces battling within someone. For example, an impatient part wanting immediate gratification might be framed as a demanding child, while a moderating part may be characterized as a strict but loving authority figure.

Over time other NLP practitioners like Robert Dilts expanded on parts work as a way to resolve inner turmoil by better integrating wisdom across these sub-personas. The concept built on psychological predecessors like Sigmund Freud's divisions of id, ego and superego as well as Internal Family Systems therapy focusing on exile and protector identities.

Steve and Connirae Andreas popularized the specific framework of "parts integration" in their book Heart of the Mind. It offered guidance on systematically uncovering disowned or disavowed aspects of oneself. By fully recognizing then negotiating between the needs of these polarized inner parts, resolution of stuck conflicts can emerge organically.

Once inner conflicts are understood as tension between differing priorities rather than threats to identity, compassionate integration towards wholeness becomes possible. Unconscious resistance drops away, aligning the mind and heart.

NLP is all about embracing the power of success and constantly enhancing techniques for ultimate efficiency. Parts Integration has undergone remarkable refinements and improvements over the years. The version we offer in our NLP training is dynamic and highly effective, providing you with practical skills you can immediately apply.

UNRESOLVED UNRESOURCEFUL EMOTIONS

Ashley was burdened by a recurring issue weighing on her for quite some time. It all started when her best friend from college, Samantha, invited her to go out with a group of friends, including a guy named Brian, whom Samantha had a crush on for quite some time. However, Ashley declined the invitation, and as a result, the plans fell through for the group. Brian ended up going out with other friends that night and met someone else, eventually starting a relationship with them. Blaming Ashley, Samantha confronted her, saying, "If you had just come out with us, Brian and I would be together but instead he found someone else. I need better friends."

Another incident that haunted Ashley's thoughts was when she was babysitting her six year old sister. Ashley had momentarily looked away to check a text message and her sister fell and broke her arm while riding her bike. Ashley blamed herself for not being more vigilant. Overwhelmed with guilt, she sobbed, remembering her mother's disappointment and the financial strain caused by the medical bills.

Ashley agonizingly replayed both incidents in her mind on a near-daily basis. At night, she would stare at the ceiling unable to quiet thoughts like "If only I had gone out with Samantha..." or "I should have watched my sister more closely." Her sleep suffered as her mind raced, imagining all the ways she could have prevented each situation.

The relentless self-blame crushed Ashley's self-confidence. Though usually very social and outgoing, she withdrew from friends and turned down invitations to parties or group events. She felt hollow and undeserving of having fun after "ruining" things for both her best friend and little sister.

When co-workers asked Ashley to join them for happy hour or summer barbecues, she made up excuses to stay home alone instead, denying herself enjoyment. Even special events like weddings provoked anxiety that something could go wrong if she attended, keeping Ashley from RSVPing.

The guilt also made Ashley overly cautious and risk-avoidant. Spontaneity faded as second-guessing dominated her decision making. She hesitated when opportunities arose like an open mic night or intramural soccer league, declining to try new things or grow through novel experiences. Her mind always jumped to "But what if something bad happens again..." trapping her in analysis paralysis.

Beyond mere guilt, Ashley struggled with a deeper shame about her actions in these painful situations.

Guilt involves feeling remorse or regret over steps taken or not taken during a specific incident. For example, guilt says "I made a mistake" or "I should have made a different choice in that moment." It critiques our behavior rather than our worthiness or essence as a person.

Shame however cuts much deeper, attacking our very identity. Shame-based inner voices declare things like "I am a failure" or "I am incompetent and don't deserve acceptance." Rather than situational regret, shame attaches a negative label to who we are at our core because of what happened.

For Ashley, her self-blame goes beyond feeling she could have acted differently. She has internalized an identity as a "bad friend" and "irresponsible sister" who ruins things for those she cares about. Her inner critic uses these events to declare she is undeserving and destroys relationships, attacking her basic worth and belongingness.

The intensity of Ashley's withdrawal and avoidance of activities she previously enjoyed indicates her self-judgment has shifted into a paralyzing shame. Until the underlying shame was healed, she continued perceiving herself as fundamentally flawed and unworthy rather than having simply made mistakes. Releasing shame was essential for Ashley to reclaim her confident, carefree spirit.

Have you ever found yourself in situations where you were made to feel guilty for something you couldn't have possibly been responsible for? Despite not having done anything wrong, you were unjustly blamed. While guilt can serve a purpose in certain situations, such as recognizing a legal or moral issue, it becomes unproductive and harmful when used to inflict negative emotions upon oneself, especially when the circumstances are beyond your control, and you played no part in the outcome.

Guilt and other related unresourceful emotions can make you feel like your past mistakes permanently define you. This false belief can lead to feelings of inferiority and inadequacy. However, it is important to remember that you deserve the love, acceptance, and compassion just for being you – a human!

In NLP we work with clients on addressing the primary emotions of anger, sadness, fear, hurt, and guilt. These primary emotions may have subsets, including anxiety, regret, shame, sorrow, and resentment, just to name a few. In NLP training, we teach our students how to focus on releasing primary emotions in their clients and then address any related subsets that may still be present.

Many people repress their emotions rather than express them, often due to learned behaviors from early experiences or a lack of safe outlets for emotional expression. Consequently, they become disconnected from their emotions and begin to generalize them, hindering their ability to learn the necessary lessons to let go of these emotions and continue their personal growth.

Avoiding unresolved emotions and leaving them unaddressed renders them unresourceful. Unresolved emotions may not feel pleasant, but they carry valuable lessons that can contribute to a better life in the long run.

By healthily resolving them, they become resources that help you unlock your progress and full potential.

Emotions can act as a thermometer for your internal state. If you find yourself experiencing an emotion that seems disproportionate to the current situation, it may indicate unresolved emotions from the past. A notable example is one we have discussed previously: when someone cuts you off in traffic, and you react with anger and hostility. It is not the other driver's action that is the root cause of your anger, but rather the emotions, anchors, and triggers within you that elicit such a reaction.

Many people search for external factors to find safety and security. When you confront these emotions head-on, you realize they are the key to unlocking your mental prison. As you work through unresolved emotions, the illusory obstacles that hindered your progress fade away, granting you genuine safety and security.

If you have unresolved emotions, you might wonder, "what can I do about them?" In the next chapter, we will look at ways to resolve these emotions.

ACCEPTANCE AND CREATING SPACE

I understand you may be going through a tough time right now, and it's natural to feel like life isn't fair. However, tough times can be beneficial. Just because something is challenging doesn't mean it's not part of the perfection in your life. Your anger, sadness, fear, hurt, and guilt are important for your growth.

Have you ever felt that life isn't fair? Well, you're absolutely right; it isn't fair! We all go through difficult situations, and acknowledging that is okay. In fact, those unfair and challenging moments in life often lead to personal growth and transformation. Remember, if it doesn't challenge you, it doesn't change you. Say that again – out loud!

We enter this world with the DNA we have to work with. Only a few individuals win the genetic lottery, being born extremely beautiful or wealthy. Others may have physical limitations, like Nick Santonastasso, one of four people with a rare genetic disorder, Hanhart Syndrome, causing him to be born without legs and with only one arm. It may seem unfair and insurmountable, but Nick hasn't let that stop him from becoming a body builder, highly sought after motivational speaker and bestselling author. He emphasizes the importance of focusing on what you have rather than dwelling on what you don't. He lives by the motto, never say you can't, ask how you can.

We are all human; no matter how blessed we may appear, even the luckiest among us face challenges. People who currently have fewer problems may encounter their share in the future. It's simply the nature of life.

We've all come across individuals born into wealth, and while it may seem like a blessing, it can also come with its own set of challenges. For example, some individuals who inherit wealth may struggle with feelings of not accomplishing anything on their own or guilt for not using the money for the greater benefit of society. Similarly, some lottery winners find that the initial excitement fades quickly as the reality of managing the money sets in. We may laugh at that reaction, but it is true. Many lottery winners have been interviewed after a period of time and often these folks are broke, depressed, and wish they had never won in the first place.

No matter your situation, the most important thing to remember is not to let these troubles bring you down. When you endure hardships without giving up and maintain a positive attitude, it builds a strong character that will serve you well as you grow older. People who have the most to be grateful for are those who have learned to find happiness in what they have. It may sound simple, but it's true! Being content with your life is a valuable trait in today's world. Instead of be limited by your challenges, challenge your limits.

It's important to recognize that fairness shouldn't be measured by what others have or don't have regarding finances, material possessions, or the life you desire. Everyone is on their unique journey, and comparing yourself to others is not a meaningful gauge of fairness. Stay focused on your own path and embrace the opportunities that come your way. Remember, you are on your own journey. Stay true to yourself and keep moving forward. Stay on your mat!

Choose to accept and love yourself fully, both inside and outside. Appreciate and embrace the unique DNA and body you have been gifted. It is the resource you have been given to fulfill your mission in life. Remember, you are no more defined by your body than by the car you drive when you sit in the driver's seat.

In yoga, there is a principle called Santosha, which translates to contentment. It is a state of being content in any situation and recognizing perfection in imperfection. True contentment comes from accepting what is in front of you and letting go of what is missing. It involves embracing life as an ongoing learning process, growing, evolving, and finding joy.

Being content doesn't mean settling for everything in your life or tolerating mediocrity. It means you stop longing for what is missing and instead appreciate what you have in the present moment. It means being okay with where you are right now. It doesn't mean ignoring goals or aspirations; rather, it suggests pursuing them with a sense of contentment along the way. It involves embracing life's ups and downs without getting overly attached to specific outcomes, recognizing that true happiness is not solely dependent on external achievements.

Learning to accept things beyond our control is a crucial aspect of contentment. When you realize that life is constantly changing and that you are continuously evolving until the end, that's when you can start accepting yourself more. This is the essence of Santosha: accepting what happens. Once we learn to be content, our minds become more focused. When we let go of the constant need for more and simply "be," we can find contentment. Paradoxically, by embracing this state of "being," we invite more positive and good things to flow into our lives.

Contentment is attractive because it means you are not constantly chasing after something external to complete you. It means you are resilient in the face of adversity, taking everything in stride and finding joy in the simple things. You might think that contentment is challenging given the current state of the world, but it is indeed possible—and it starts with you.

The practice of Santosha is simple. First, pay attention to the world around you. Notice the taste of fresh fruit, feel the sun's warmth on your skin, and appreciate the loving gaze of your dog when you return home from work. Take in the world's beauty because there are countless things you may miss if you don't. The most important thing is to savor each moment you have. Remember that life is a journey encompassing both sad and happy times. With Santosha, you learn to accept the ups and downs, find joy in the journey, and trust that there is always light at the end of the tunnel. Every moment is a blessing.

Take a moment to reflect on your life. What do you desire more of? Happiness? Peace? Love? Whatever it may be, create a list of actions to move yourself closer to that path. If you seek happiness, engage in activities that bring you joy. If you long for more peace, incorporate routines and practices into your daily life that promote serenity. It all starts with your mindset. Believe that you deserve what you desire and that you have the power to make it happen.

Creating Space for Your Emotions

We must fully embrace our emotions. When we accept and fully embrace our emotions, we often discover a feeling of love on the other side. Accepting our emotions takes away their charge and allows us to appreciate them. On the other hand, when we judge our emotions and wish they weren't there, we create resistance, and instead they persist. To move through emotions and find the learning and love beyond them, we need to create space for them. If we have trained our subconscious mind to always protect us from "negative" emotions, we risk missing out on the experience of emotions all together. Emotions are necessary for learning and growth.

As Carl Jung wisely said, "What you resist not only persists but will grow in size." When we resist suppressed emotions from the past, they continue to persist. This happens because where attention goes, energy flows, as discussed in

Chapter 4 regarding the principle of Makia. We give them attention and energy by resisting unresolved emotions, preventing them from being resolved. Therefore, we must intentionally create space for them.

You might wonder, what does it mean to create space for emotions? Creating space for emotions is like "holding space" for another person, as taught by coaches, mental health professionals, and holistic practitioners. However, in this case, you are holding space for your emotions.

You are present with your emotions without judgment when you hold space for them. You observe them with an open heart, without expecting what you should say or do. You practice empathy, compassion, and acceptance of your emotions, allowing yourself to just be.

In our mindfulness training, I teach the practice of holding space for others. It is an invaluable skill that allows us to be truly present for another person. When we hold space for someone, we connect with them deeply, seeing them more clearly and understanding them fully. Holding space for emotions is a similar process. By holding space for your emotions, you can feel seen, understood, and cared for by yourself. I highly recommend you take our mindfulness training, if for no other reason than to learn to hold space for others.

Here are some ways you can practice acceptance and create space for your emotions:

1. Taking deep breaths is a powerful way to stay connected to yourself. Earlier in this book, we discussed the Vagus Nerve and its connection to breathing. Practicing meditation and entering a reflective, meditative state can help set the environment for this connection. By doing so, you can connect with yourself on a deeper level. For example, when you feel overwhelmed, stressed, or anxious, take deep breaths and reestablish that connection within yourself.

2. Find a comfortable place where you will not be disturbed, close your eyes, and allow the emotion you accept to come up. It is natural for the mind to try to eliminate uncomfortable experiences. Instead, allow the emotion to be present within you.

3. Observe without judgment. This step is crucial, as judging the arising emotion can be tempting. For example, if the emotion is "hurt," simply allow that emotion to come up and observe it. Avoid labeling it as good or bad, right or wrong. Have no opinion of it. Just observe.

4. Avoid the urge to solve it. Your initial instinct might be to minimize the situation, solve the issue, or reframe the emotion, and that is not the purpose of creating space. Instead, transition back to sitting with the emotion and observing it.

5. Detach yourself. It is easier to understand something when we can attach it to ourselves. However, the focus is on the emotion itself in creating space for emotions. Observe it without attachment.

6. Recognize the thoughts that arise, the sensations in your body, and the critical inner voice that often accompanies the emotion.

7. Notice the emotional experience within the body. Observe what you feel and identify all the points in your body where you can sense this emotion.

8. Pay attention to the details of the emotion, such as its size, color, temperature, and shape. As you explore the characteristics of this particular emotion, be cautious not to chase the object of the emotion. There is no need to search for a reason or source; simply stay present with the emotion.

9. Notice the more you move toward the emotion, the more elusive it becomes. It is changing and in motion, similar to thoughts. This emotion is energy, always part of a grand flow. Observing it, instead of grasping it or identifying with it, gives the emotion the freedom to transform, move, and even dissipate because the emotion is not who you are. It is simply energy within your body.

Learning to accept unconsciously held emotions is crucial, and creating space is the first step. As a practitioner, my next step is to use T.I.M.E. techniques.

T.I.M.E. Techniques

 T.I.M.E. stands for Time Integration for Maximum Empowerment. T.I.M.E. is a powerful set of techniques that easily and effortlessly eliminates unresolved emotions.

These techniques guide us to make better decisions, set and achieve positive goals, and ultimately improve our lives. In our NLP certification training, we teach T.I.ME. techniques and instruct coaches on how to conduct one-on-one coaching sessions to guide clients through the process.

The foundation of time techniques can be traced back to 1890 when William James mentioned them in his book, Principles of Psychology. James theorized that the unconscious mind linearly stores memories, following a timeline. Over time, contributions from psychologists and practitioners in the field of NLP, such as Fritz Perls and others, further supported the positive impact of these techniques.

The underlying premise of T.I.M.E techniques is that everyone organizes their memories and future expectations uniquely, creating their personal timeline. This timeline represents the flow of time within us, with the past extending in one direction, the future in another, and the present moment positioned somewhere in between. The orientation of your timeline holds some importance, as it influences how you perceive time, make decisions, and experience life as a whole.

The Impact of T.I.M.E Techniques

When it comes to practitioner techniques for growth and change, T.I.M.E techniques are in a league of their own. While talk therapy and visualization can provide intellectual insights or imagined scenarios, T.I.M.E operates at the neurological core.

By directly interfacing with memories and emotions lodged in the subconscious mind, T.I.M.E techniques create deep recalibration. It's like a software update for the psyche. Limiting patterns that once defined a person's reality are overwritten with new positive resources.

Other modalities rely on conscious analysis or willpower to spur change. But these are confined to the rational mind and eventually exhaust mental resources. TIME aligns the conscious and subconscious minds for long-term transformation.

When we teach T.I.M.E a key involves learning to assist the client in connecting with their timeline upon which life memories are sequentially stored. As mentioned, this timeline is comprised of a past extending behind one's current vantage point, a future ahead, and the present moment situated in between.

Then, the practitioner assists in finding the root cause of the unresolved emotion and finally assists the client in releasing that emotion.

You could describe the experience of T.I.M.E techniques as "emotional renovation" - the foundations don't change but the interior is upgraded. Neural pathways are rewired, beliefs are reframed, and new potential is unlocked.

People then possess the power to break free from the gravitational pull of past pain, doubts and obstacles. They are able to design futures where anything is possible, unencumbered by illusions of limitation.

No other methodology penetrates the subconscious fortress in the precise way T.I.M.E techniques do. For this reason, T.I.M.E enables change that is both deeper and more permanent than other approaches. It empowers people to radically reinvent themselves at the neurological source. T.I.M.E techniques clear the way for enormous growth by resolving emotional blocks from one's history. Limiting beliefs represent false constraints regarding one's identity and capabilities. Now that we've explored T.I.M.E techniques for emotional resolution, we can turn our attention to limiting beliefs, another major inner obstacle that can be transformed.

LIMITING BELIEFS

Have you ever found yourself self-sabotaging your efforts to achieve a goal? Have you tried various approaches, but nothing seems to work? If you feel stuck in repetitive patterns and unsure of how to break free, it's likely that underlying limiting beliefs are holding you back from reaching your full potential. The first step to overcoming these beliefs is to recognize and dismantle the illusion they create.

Our subconscious mind often guides our actions without our conscious awareness. Our beliefs shape our identity and influence our actions. For example, when we believe in our potential for success, we are more motivated to take action. Conversely, when we doubt ourselves or lack faith in our abilities, we give up before even trying, hindering our progress and limiting our success. By becoming aware of these limiting beliefs, we can work on transforming them to align with the person we aspire to be.

Limiting beliefs can manifest in various forms, such as "I am too old," "I am not good enough," or "there is never enough." Perhaps you have encountered these beliefs from others or even spoken them to yourself. It's important to recognize that we all experience limiting beliefs at some point, but the good news is that they can be eliminated effortlessly and easily.

Limiting beliefs can be about anything. They can pertain to ourselves, others, or the world. They act as barriers, preventing us from having what we desire, becoming who we want to be, and pursuing our true potential. Although these beliefs may defy logic and even be unhealthy or irrational, we often hold onto them tightly out of familiarity. As we gain new experiences and create new memories, we no longer need to cling to beliefs that no longer serve us.

Throughout our life journey, we acquire these limiting beliefs based on our memories, personal truths, experiences, emotions, and interpretations. Many of these beliefs are formed during childhood and have persisted, becoming self-fulfilling prophecies if left unaddressed. Often subconsciously, these beliefs shape our perception of reality, trapping us in limited states of mind until we become aware of them.

It is crucial to understand that we have the power to create our future through the thoughts we choose, the language we use, the decisions we make, and the actions we take. By challenging and transforming our limiting beliefs, we open ourselves to new possibilities and create a pathway to personal growth and fulfillment.

Your beliefs play a significant role in shaping your future because they influence the decisions and actions you take. When you hold onto limiting beliefs, you make choices that confine you and create a limited life. Therefore, it's important to reflect on what you believe is holding you back from taking the necessary actions to achieve the results you desire in life.

Recognize that your beliefs present an opportunity for extraordinary transformation and fulfillment. The more a belief appears to be true to you, the more power it holds over you. Therefore, I encourage you to stop fighting for your limiting beliefs and instead break through them to pave a path of positive action and decisions.

In our household, my wife, Theresa, and I regularly apply these techniques to ourselves, holding each other accountable. Leading by example is our guiding principle. When we encounter a limiting belief, we ask the empowering question, "When did you decide that?". This question prompts the subconscious mind to delve deep and brings awareness to the moment you accept a limitation in your life. Even if you can't consciously recall the exact date and time, your subconscious knows, and it triggers you to think consciously about when and why you first embraced that belief. The words we use, both internally and externally, hold great importance. While we teach and utilize these techniques regularly, we acknowledge that personal growth is an ongoing journey for all of us.

Another version of this question is, "What makes you choose to believe that?"

This question is incredibly important because it helps us uncover the underlying reasons behind our limiting beliefs. By asking ourselves, "What makes you choose to believe that?", we are challenging the validity of our beliefs and opening ourselves up to the possibility of change and growth.

With both questions, when we examine the reasons why we choose to believe certain things, we gain a clearer understanding of the influences and experiences that have shaped our perspectives. It allows us to question the validity of those influences and determine if they still serve us in our present lives.

Asking this question helps us take ownership of our beliefs. It reminds us that belief is a choice, and we have the power to choose differently. It empowers us to challenge societal norms, cultural expectations, and even our own self-imposed limitations.

When we consciously explore the reasons behind our beliefs, we create space for new possibilities and opportunities. We open ourselves up to new perspectives, ideas, and ways of being. We become more adaptable, resilient, and open-minded.

I myself felt overwhelmed recently as I reviewed my planned activities during my morning routine for the day. With multiple ventures, projects, and a home renovation underway, I thought, "I just can't fit all of this into today. There are more tasks on my list than hours in the day." While discussing the plans for the day, Theresa asked me, with a slight grin, "When did you decide that?". It made me pause and realize: I was holding a limiting belief. At that moment, I started using some of the same empowering questions I teach my clients:

- What if it were possible?
- Do I need to do everything in one day?
- What if I could accomplish it all?
- Is there a solution? Can I reschedule or delegate tasks?
- How can I complete as much as possible?
- How can I be a solution?

Theresa looked at my list and offered to handle two tasks for me. It may seem simple, but that one question dissolved the limiting belief, and a solution emerged. This example illustrates a surface-level limiting belief, but how often do we allow deep-rooted beliefs to shape our lives? How often do we believe our lies because we have held onto them for an extended period?

It's time to challenge those beliefs and create a new narrative that aligns with your true potential. By asking empowering questions and exploring alternative perspectives, you can break free from the constraints of limiting beliefs and open a world of possibilities.

If you would like to dive a little deeper into limiting beliefs and learn the process for breaking through them, take advantage of our free resource Breaking Limiting Beliefs, that is available to you at our website. It walks you through the process of breaking through those beliefs that have been holding you back in life.

https://destinyrising.net/breakingbeliefs

Attachments

Attachment, seen as a form of dependence, often creates an illusion of happiness. Many believe their happiness derives from external sources such as other people, external circumstances, or material possessions. Consequently, when something goes wrong with these sources, they become anxious about losing them. And when a change does occur, such as losing a job, possession, ending a relationship, or relocating, they can be overwhelmed by grief and other unresourceful emotions. We tend to develop strong attachments to those who bring us joy because we mistakenly believe we need them to be happy and fear losing them.

However, true happiness goes beyond illusion when we recognize that we don't need people or things to make us happy. Instead, we realize we are complete and can experience full happiness without relying on external factors. There is nothing inherently wrong with finding joy in relationships, people, or things. The key is understanding that the happiness we derive from them stems from gratitude and appreciation, creating genuine happiness. People and things are not prerequisites for our contentment. Adopting this mindset allows us to experience true happiness, whether or not the people or things we desire are present in our lives.

We open ourselves to happiness when we let go of the need to control people, situations, and outcomes. Letting go is crucial because it grants us the freedom to experience joy. By releasing our attachment to specific outcomes, we allow people and things to fulfill us without giving them the power to destroy us.

Attachment to people is a common phenomenon. We often hear phrases like "this is my better half." In movies, we encounter scenes where characters declare, "You complete me." While these expressions may sound romantic, the truth is that each of us is already whole and complete as an individual. We don't need someone else to complete or fulfill us. It's natural to feel deeply connected and close to another person. Such feelings can be healthy for a relationship if we recognize the importance of maintaining our individuality. However, beliefs such as "I live for him/her," or "I can't live without them" can be unhealthy. Letting go of someone we care deeply for can be challenging, especially if we believe our happiness depends on them. Yet, these thoughts are illusions we create. They are not rooted and are reinforced by limiting beliefs. If we acknowledge our strength and resilience in navigating life changes, it becomes easier to let go of those limiting beliefs and experience less pain.

When we love someone unconditionally, our love should not be contingent on what we expect in return. Instead, it should be based on how much we are willing to give without any expectations. Unconditional love means appreciating and enjoying someone's company for who they truly are without pressuring them to meet our expectations or conform to an idealized image.

Creating a strong relationship with yourself is crucial. It involves being comfortable spending time alone and genuinely enjoying that time to yourself. Do you truly know yourself as well as you think you do? Take a moment to reflect on that question. If the answer isn't a resounding "yes," it's time to dedicate some effort to getting to know yourself better. Invest time in developing interests that hold personal meaning and align with your values and passions. These interests should stem from within you rather than being influenced by external expectations or the desire to meet others' standards.

For example, suppose your sense of worthiness, completeness, confidence, or goodness depends solely on receiving compliments or positive feedback from others. In that case, it becomes much harder to let go of those individuals when necessary. Instead, believe in your own worthiness regardless of external validation or opinions. This way, you can relate to people as individuals, appreciating them for who they are rather than viewing them solely as a reflection of your self-worth.

Releasing attachment to others grants them freedom, too. It allows them to be authentic and give of themselves uniquely without the pressure to meet your expectations or become someone you want them to be. This fosters a more fulfilling and genuine form of love than attachment-based relationships could ever create.

Attachment To Emotions

When we experience emotions, our minds often label them as positive or negative. Positive emotions become desired experiences that we seek to repeat, sometimes leading to addiction to those emotions. Negative emotions can also become addictive and trigger the brain's reward centers. Regularly indulging in negative emotions deceive our brain into thinking it's being rewarded. Worry, regret, disappointment, pride, shame, and guilt can activate the brain's reward centers, creating an illusion of relief or familiarity. It may even feel comforting to dwell in these negative emotions and believe they define who we are, trapping us in a single moment. However, it's essential to recognize that these feelings do not define us. We are much more than the sum of our parts, and holding onto these negative emotions only hinders our personal growth and well-being.

Dr. Joe Dispenza discusses how our brains frequently activate the fight or flight response when we perceive threats. For instance, receiving a curt email or text from a partner triggers the release of chemicals such as cortisol and adrenaline, preparing us to deal with the potentially threatening situation. As a result, our focus narrows to the outer world, our identities, and our environment. This response is helpful when facing danger in a natural setting, such as encountering a bear during a hike. In those instances, the heightened state subsides once the threat is gone, and our neurological chemistry returns to balance. However, we often find ourselves entering the fight or flight mode regularly due to various situations like conflicts with coworkers, arguments with spouses, unexpected messages, or encountering something that evokes negative emotions.

When the threat persists, our chemistry remains in heightened arousal. The trigger is always present, such as sitting next to a challenging coworker's desk or constantly being within reach of phone notifications. Prolonged imbalances can lead to a chronically stimulated state, potentially resulting in mental or physical illness. It is possible to become addicted to these chemicals because our brains become accustomed to their frequent release. Like a drug addict seeking a fix, despite knowing it is unhealthy, we may crave these chemicals as we strive to increase our chances of survival by forcing outcomes. The more we engage in this behavior, the stronger the addiction becomes.

When our bodies experience constant stress, our brains go into overdrive to ensure our safety. Our focus is narrowed and we concentrate on potential threats or people, meticulously analyzing every detail to determine the safest action. People all react different to stress. Some people experience tunnel vision during panic attacks or traumatic events. Those with extreme anxiety or paranoia may display physical symptoms like rapid eye movement, constantly scanning for threats, and assessing their surroundings from every possible viewpoint. This constant state of fight, flight, or freeze can be mentally and physically exhausting.

Finding joy in life often stems from living in the present moment. When we constantly fear the future, dwell on the past, or remain in a heightened state, it becomes challenging to experience happiness in the present. Letting go of familiar emotions and triggers can be daunting, but it is also liberating. It empowers us to take calculated risks, try new things, and fully embrace everything life offers.

Attachment To the Past

In the words of Jimmy Buffett, "Oh, yesterdays are over my shoulder, so I can't look back for too long. There's just too much to see waiting in front of me, and I know that I just can't go wrong."

We previously discussed the labels others put on us, and we put on ourselves, which can tie us to the past. Statements like "I am shy," "I am not a good speaker," or "I am not a business person" are limiting beliefs rooted in past decisions. However, since you can make choices, you can also make new choices now. It's possible that you lacked proper training or effective strategies in the past. Still, you can change your language and say, "I am approaching people more confidently." Remember, identities and labels can attach us to the past or create our future. You have the power to create your future.

Emotion creates anchors to past events. Perhaps you have a memory that you constantly relive. Remember our minds distort and generalize events. How you remember something may not reflect exactly how it happened. Our brains seek patterns and order to help us make decisions that protect us from danger. When something negative occurs, it disrupts our existing order and introduces chaos. Our brains naturally try to return to the event's site and make sense of it to restore order to our world.

Your power lies in the present moment, where action takes place. Your actions today shape your tomorrow. Instead of dwelling on past hurts or struggles, focus on the lessons learned and apply them in the present. The future is merely imagined, while the past exists only in our distorted memories. Your true power lies in the present moment, free from the influence of the past or the future. Concentrate on your passions, values, and what you love.

Take a positive and creative step today, no matter how small. Be impactful in this present moment by releasing what lies within you. Enroll in a class, learn a new skill, help someone in need, create a course, write a book – Do anything positive, just take action! Seize the moment of now. As Bil Keane said, "Yesterday's the past, tomorrow's the future, but today is a gift. That's why it's called the present."

Since today is yesterday's tomorrow, today will be tomorrow's yesterday, so get busy!

Attachment To Outcomes

Sarah had been arguing with her mom for weeks about whether to send her kids to private school. The arguments were sometimes heated, leading Sarah and her mom to go days without speaking. After a recent intense argument, they stopped talking for over a week. Finally, Sarah's mom called and expressed how much she missed her, suggesting they meet for lunch. Sarah agreed and intended to work things out and find peace.

Despite her mom's harsh words, Sarah understood they came from a place of love and concern for her grandchildren. As Sarah drove to the restaurant, she visualized a peaceful lunch where they would apologize to each other and agree to disagree. During the conversation at lunch, Sarah apologized, and her mom accepted, appreciating Sarah's dedication to raising her children and acknowledging her as a good mom.

However, Sarah expected an apology for the hurtful words spoken a week ago, which didn't come. As they left, Sarah snarked, "Well, if you can't apologize, then I guess we have nothing to discuss." She got in her car and left, losing sight of her intention for peace because she was attached to a very specific outcome.

I love using a technique with my clients where I guide them to visualize an outcome in their future. This powerful tool works on both conscious and subconscious levels.

However, one crucial aspect we teach is letting go of the outcome after setting it. You must remain open to the intended outcome or something even better entering your life. This is why setting clear intentions is essential. For instance, let's say you set an intention to find love and meet your ideal partner, envisioning someone with blonde hair, blue eyes, driving a specific car, and living in a particular neighborhood. This becomes your intention—to meet and fall in love with that person. Then, you meet someone who has brown eyes instead of blue. If you are focused on the intention, you will have an open mind and give this individual a chance. However, if you are attached to the outcome, you may dismiss them, thinking they are not the right person for you. You limit your opportunities by staying fixated on the outcome rather than the intention.

Being attached to a specific outcome can create an illusionary obstacle that happiness can only be achieved someday when everything aligns perfectly. However, true happiness lies in the present moment by having gratitude for what you have and where you are now. There is no moment more deserving of your happiness than now because it's the only moment that truly exists.

This doesn't mean you can't actively work towards creating your future. Instead, it means finding peace with the present moment, without feeling that something is wrong with you or your life, and operating from a place of acceptance. The beauty of setting an intention is that it starts in the now. You don't have to wait to start a business, pursue a relationship, finish a course, or achieve any other outcome. Intention begins in the present moment and guides you through all aspects of your life. Set intentions for your relationships, health, finances, work, and every area of your life.

FEAR

"Fear is not real. The only place where fear can exist is our thoughts of the future. It is the product of our imagination, causing us to fear things that do not currently exist and may never exist. That is near insanity. Now, do not misunderstand me, danger is very real, but fear is a choice."

- Will Smith, After Earth.

Fear is an unresolved emotion that often stems from three obstacles: unresourceful emotions, limiting beliefs and/or decisions, and internal conflicts. Any of these can be tied to attachments to people, things, emotions, or the past.

The amygdala, a small part of the brain often referred to as the reptilian brain, generates fear. It is responsible for helping us navigate away from danger. Humans are born with only two innate fears: the fear of falling and the fear of loud noises. However, research shows that everything else is a learned fear.

Healthy fears are known as primal fears. Theses healthy fears protect us from real dangers that could lead to harm or death. An example of primal fear is feeling fear when crossing a busy intersection with no crosswalk and seeing a speeding car. Primal fears exist to keep us safe.

Most fears we experience throughout our lives are learned fears acquired during our developmental stages. Have you ever feared something that never actually happened? Have you worried excessively about a future event that never came to pass? If so, you have experienced fear's companion: anxiety.

Although we are born with only two fears, our learned fears often hinder our progress in life. These illusory fears can be categorized into three main types: 1. The fear of not being accepted, 2. The fear of not being loved, and 3. The fear of suffering. Despite their simplicity, these are the underlying realities of most fears. Denis Waitley's backronym for FEAR - False Education Appearing Real - succinctly captures this concept.

Society plays a significant role in conditioning us to fear. Fear is frequently used to foster conformity in various contexts, such as political parties, campaigns, or social movements. People employ fear to manipulate others into aligning with their beliefs by implying that not doing so will result in a significantly worse life. This fear-mongering aims to make individuals believe that a different opinion is inherently wrong.

Fear is often accompanied by two related emotions: guilt and shame. Guilt arises when we believe we have done something wrong or hurtful to others. Shame is feeling inadequacy, believing we are not good, lovable, kind, or smart enough.

Fear served a crucial purpose in the past when our ancestors needed to be cautious about potential threats while searching for food. As social creatures, human beings rely on interaction and belonging to survive. Being cast out from the tribe often led to death, so emotions like guilt and shame acted as warning signals, alerting us when our behavior may jeopardize our acceptance within our chosen communities. Likewise, when we feel we have misbehaved, our brains release stress hormones that motivate us to improve our behavior.

The society also utilizes shame and guilt to foster conformity. Our families, friends, and the media have conditioned us to these emotions. For instance, we've likely encountered statements such as, "If you don't display this sign in your yard, you should be ashamed of yourself," or "If you don't align with our group's beliefs, then you lack sympathy for those who suffer."

Unfortunately, many individuals have been conditioned to fear, hurt, and guilt during their upbringing. Parents may unknowingly project their own fears and beliefs onto their children. For example, a child might be told they must attend college to secure a good job. In addition, parents may unintentionally guilt children into conforming to societal expectations by asserting that the child's actions might not make the family proud if they don't follow the parents' plan. While this may seem absurd to some, it is a reality for others. We often see individuals shamed and told they won't succeed unless they conform to certain expectations. It's important to remember the NLP presupposition, people are doing the best they can with the resources they have available. Still, the lack of resources can lead to negative emotions and lifelong guilt or shame when the child's values conflict with those projected onto them.

Of course, parents do not intend to inflict this projection of fear onto their children. On the contrary, they believe they are helping. The fear is disguised as love, hiding in a Trojan horse that goes unnoticed.

Fear acts as a catalyst for war many times through the fear of the unknown. It fuels the fear of a country being attacked or acting preemptively, the fear of death is in many ways the fear of the unknown. This fear perpetuates a cycle of violence as people try to protect themselves by attacking others first, believing it will prevent harm. In reality, this only sustains a cycle of violence.

Fear also serves as a catalyst for hatred. People fear what they do not know or understand, contributing to racism and xenophobia. The fear of the unknown and creating an "us versus them" mentality play significant roles in these dynamics.

Learning to manage and overcome fear is one of the most important skills one can acquire. Fears, like other unresolved emotions, keep us from living the life we desire and experiencing new possibilities.

Interestingly, researchers at Cornell University conducted a long-term study and discovered that 85% of what humans fear and worry about never happens. Therefore, what truly holds us back from our dreams is an illusion. However, the success we imagine is more real than the fears that are mere illusions.

In fact, fear is nothing more than an illusion created by our limiting beliefs. We are not truly afraid of failure or rejection. Instead, we resist trying new things because we fear not being good enough. We believe if we fail, we won't be accepted or loved. This keeps us within the confines of our comfort zones, where we don't have to risk "failure." This belief, however, is an illusion, because we are good enough and loved.

Fear signals that we are stepping out of our comfort zone and venturing into the unknown. Unfortunately, our minds subconsciously perceive this as a potential danger linked to the possibility of death. However, learning to interpret fear differently can become empowering, as it signifies our willingness to push beyond our limits.

Many people perceive success as an unattainable goal, which leads to fear when attempting things outside their comfort zone. The truth is that success is often built upon what is commonly called "failure." Failure, in reality, is nothing more than an illusionary obstacle. If we examine the success stories of accomplished individuals, we'll find that their journeys are comprised of numerous "failures" and setbacks. What distinguishes these individuals is how they handle these perceived failures. Do they give up or do they persist and learn from the experience? Successful people continue their efforts until they achieve success. They don't let fear dictate their actions. They use feedback to their advantage. By embracing a growth mindset, you can view every apparent failure as a stepping stone toward success. You can even anticipate and welcome the feedback that guides you toward achievement.

Remember the NLP principle we discussed earlier: there is no failure, only feedback. When you view results as feedback, you can learn from the outcomes and adjust your approach until you achieve the desired or even better result. This mindset shift can lead to greater success in all aspects of life, not just in business. Feedback is simply life's way of prompting you to try something different. Two powerful techniques to transition from failure to feedback involve reflecting on past instances where you perceived failure and writing them down. Then, replace the word "failure" with "feedback."

I spoke with James, who was once very successful with webinars. His audience grew from a small group of 5-10 people to over 100 attendees per session. Curious about why he had stopped conducting webinars despite their success, I asked him about it. James replied, "I can't continue to be successful with them anymore. They have become too big." I inquired, "When did you decide that?" James explained, "Well, after the last two webinars, I considered them failures. I was extremely nervous and distracted during the presentations, and they didn't go well. I also failed to realize that the room was capped at 100 participants, and messages poured in. It was a mess. I'm afraid to do another one because I fear messing up and damaging my reputation. So I'm sticking with other media options," he concluded with a sense of discouragement.

While various NLP tools and techniques could assist James, let's consider what he could have done for himself. He could have written down his perceived failures on paper and replaced the word "failure" with "feedback."

Example:

Failure

"I faced a challenge setting up that web meeting because the room had a maximum capacity of 100 people, and I wasn't aware of it."

Transformed into feedback...

"I received feedback that the platform I used for the web meeting has a cap on the number of participants, limiting it to 100 people. I wasn't aware of this restriction, which required additional resources and time for setup. Moving forward, I will ensure I set up future meetings accordingly. Wow, I had 100 people in my presentation?!"

Next, you take the learnings from the feedback, apply them, and move forward.

Whenever things deviate from the planned course, it's essential to ask yourself, "What can I learn from this situation?"

Allow yourself space to reflect on what didn't go as planned without passing judgment, and consider how to apply these learnings in the future. By taking a step back and exploring your options, you'll be better prepared to navigate future challenges.

Remember Carl Jung's wise words, "What you resist not only persists but will grow in size." When you resist something, you've learned to fear in the past, that fear tends to persist. In essence, you end up attracting more of what you don't want. This is because fear doesn't arise from the person, situation, or action, but from resistance.

The most effective way to overcome fear is to create space for it and then utilize the NLP T.I.M.E techniques discussed earlier. Feel the fear, acknowledge its presence, refrain from judging it, and express gratitude. Your unconscious mind is communicating something to you, attempting to protect you. Take a moment to thank your unconscious mind and say, "Thank you, unconscious mind, for these valuable learnings. I don't need the emotion of fear to protect me. I recognize that true protection in life comes from the lessons I've gained!"

When you find yourself in disagreement with the reality around you, it is easy to become trapped in negative emotions and resist what you're witnessing. Remember to ask yourself "what am I willing to accept?". Taking a step back and recognizing your perspective may not be entirely accurate (considering how we filter things) can help you move forward from the situation. This resistance stems from a desire to avoid the painful aspects of the experience. By attending our Create Your Future events or other live training sessions, you'll learn techniques in person to eliminate fear and extract the learnings without resistance or becoming attached to the past. In the meantime, here are some insightful questions to journal and gain clarity about your fears:

- What am I resisting?
- What would courage look like in this situation?
- What is the dominant force at play here - fear or courage?
- How is this fear serving me? (Do you believe it is protecting you in some way? Remember, we don't need the emotion of fear to protect us. The truth is, the things that truly protect us in life are the lessons we learn.)
- What would my future-self-advise me?
- Am I truly facing a life-or-death situation with this person or event?

By exploring these questions, you'll better understand your fears and how they influence your perspective. It will empower you to make conscious choices and embrace courage in facing challenges. Remember, fear is often an illusion that holds us back, and the path to growth lies in transforming fear into learning and stepping into a more empowered future.

Once you have explored your emotions through journaling, the next step is learning to create space for them.

CALM

My wife and I were boating on the lake one afternoon and stumbled upon a small beach. We decided to beach the pontoon and soak in the day's beauty. The trees created a perfect reflection in the calm water, resembling a flawless mirror. Even the sky mirrored itself, creating an incredible duplicate image. The wake of passing boats occasionally disrupted the reflection with gentle ripples, but it would quickly settle back into its calm state. We marveled at the beauty before us for about an hour.

However, as the afternoon progressed, clouds began to roll in, signaling an impending change in the weather. The once-perfect reflection distorted, and then the rain fell. The reflection became unrecognizable with each raindrop, and the downpour intensifying. Our lives mirror this phenomenon. When things are calm, we can see a clear reflection of what is happening around us. When waves come crashing in, there is distortion, and clarity becomes nearly impossible.

How can you find more calmness? How can you clear the water that distorts your reality? In our trainings, we teach various techniques including emotional freedom techniques, uptime vision, and the concept of vagal tone.

What exactly is vagal tone? Is it the name of a Las Vegas band? Not quite. It refers to the tone of your Vagus Nerve. The vagus nerve connects the brain to the body and regulates involuntary functions like heart rate. Strengthening vagal tone activates the relaxation response.

If you notice its resemblance to the word "vagabond," it is because they share the same root. The term "vagus" comes from Latin, meaning "to wander." the Vagus Nerve, a long nerve extending from the brainstem to the abdomen, plays a significant role in the body. It is part of the parasympathetic nervous system, responsible for involuntary actions and activities. For example, the Vagus Nerve influences the fight-or-flight response, heart rate, blood pressure, digestive processes, and other involuntary functions. Acting as a messenger, it carries information to and from the brain, taking in sensory information and transmitting it to the brain. The brain then processes and responds to that information, sending instructions to the body through the Vagus Nerve on how to function.

Increasing your vagal tone activates the relaxation response, enabling your body to recover from stress more efficiently. Higher vagal tone has also been associated with positive emotions and better physical health. By enhancing your vagal tone, you can improve both your physical and mental well-being.

How can you increase your vagal tone? Here are four effective techniques:

1. **Breathe deeply:** taking slow and deep breaths is a powerful method to activate your Vagus Nerve, reducing anxiety and enhancing the parasympathetic system. Most

people breathe at a rate of 10-14 breaths per minute, but deliberately slowing down to 6 breaths per minute can stimulate the Vagus Nerve and induce relaxation. Focus on deep inhalations from your diaphragm, allowing your stomach to expand. Exhale slowly and evenly. Box breathing, which involves inhaling, holding, exhaling, and holding again in equal counts, can be helpful.

2. **Cold exposure:** acute cold exposure, such as cold plunges, cold showers or exposure to cold air, can offer numerous benefits. It can improve mood, promote relaxation, aid in weight loss, increase energy levels, boost the immune system, reduce inflammation, and enhance metabolism. Cold exposure can also contribute to better sleep. Start with 30 seconds of cold water at the end of your shower and gradually increase the exposure over time.

3. **Meditation:** meditation practices can help relax both the body and mind, leading to increased vagal tone. Meditation reduces the activity of the sympathetic "fight or flight" response and increases vagal modulation. In addition, research indicates that meditation can elevate positive emotions, including self-compassion.

4. **Massage:** massages have been found to impact the Vagus Nerve, resulting in increased vagal activity and vagal tone. Specific areas of the body can be targeted to stimulate the Vagus Nerve. For example, foot massages (reflexology) and massaging the carotid sinus near the right side of the throat can activate the Vagus Nerve and potentially reduce seizures. Another simple technique involves placing your

index finger at the bottom of the inside of your ear and gently pinching the ear with your thumb. Massage the area in circular motions, approximately 10 times in one direction and then 10 times in the opposite direction. Once vagal tone is strengthened through these methods, we can approach life from an empowered state.

LOVE

You can make decisions based on unresourceful emotions or approach them from a higher state of love. Love is an incredibly potent energy that enables transformation and creation. While many positive heightened emotions exist, such as joy, peace, gratitude, confidence, and relaxation, love is the most powerful.

To enhance your creative energy of abundance and freedom, it is advisable to reprogram any habits that hinder your progress. These habits may include finding faults in situations and others, both in your internal thoughts and your words. Remember that everyone is doing their best with the resources available to them, and they are following their own unique paths in life.

Often, people fall into destructive patterns of behavior that hold them back from achieving their goals. If you desire a more positive and productive life, you must let go of negativity, pessimism, judgment, and cynicism, as they only obstruct your creative energy. Gossiping is also a habit that should be reprogrammed to open yourself up to greater possibilities and success. Instead, focus on speaking words of positivity, acceptance, and love. Habits are learned behaviors that become ingrained through repetition. By cultivating awareness and making a conscious effort, you can reprogram your habits to be more positive and optimistic. Condition yourself to process your worldview with love, fierce kindness, peace, and positivity.

Within every obstacle lies an opportunity. Embrace the best version of yourself!

NEXT STEPS

Remember, these techniques are for personal use only. You are not yet certified to work with others. If you or anyone, including yourself, has a medically diagnosable condition, seeking professional licensed medical assistance is always important.

If you want to connect with like-minded individuals dedicated to creating their futures and positively impacting others' lives, our live training is perfect for you! NLP has been utilized by top professionals in various fields. Our training programs teach the techniques in an easily understandable manner, allowing you to initiate meaningful change in people's lives and even explore new career paths. It's time to move towards greater achievements and fulfillment. We invite you to join us and learn how to make a positive difference for yourself, your friends, your family, and the world.

Our Personal Development Coaching, Hypnosis, and Neuro-Linguistic Programming courses are certified by the International Board of Coaches and Practitioners (IBCP). This non-profit organization upholds the standards and ethics of these disciplines. Graduates of our courses are eligible for certification through IBCP as well. Contact us to find out more about our live training by going to www.destinyrising.net/contact

www.ingramcontent.com/pod-product-compliance
Lightning Source LLC
Chambersburg PA
CBHW060515030426
42337CB00015B/1901